About the Author

Throughout the course of his youth and adult life George has been focused on the interface between the psychology of Carl Jung and Christian spirituality. This has been expressed first in priestly ministry and spiritual direction, and now in psychotherapy, counselling, peace and nonviolence education and artwork. George is committed to promoting Jung's psychological insights as contemporary spiritual practice for the wellbeing of individuals and for the common good. He lives in Western Australia.

georgetrippe@gmail.com
website: TrippeArt.com

Testimonial statements

How did I get here? It's a great question. It is provocative through and through.

The Revd. Gary Commins, PhD

This is a very useful piece of work and I have benefited greatly from reading it a couple of times. This is a wonderful workbook/ study guide to engage in a reflective process.

Brendan McKeague

The sharing of his personal stories encouraged me to reflect and to self-examine.

Dr. Louis Papaelias

What an incredible privilege. I am certain I will return to this work at many points throughout my life.

Timothy McInnes

A truly insightful piece of writing that has significantly changed my approach to the way I live my life.

Adrian Pizzata

The work, both insightful and provocative, opens a door for those seeking to explore the undiscovered dimensions of the inner world.

Stephen Harrison, DMin

How Did I Get Here?

Reflecting on my principles for nonviolent living

George E. Trippe, PhD

First published 2022 by George E. Trippe, PhD

Produced by Independent Ink
independentink.com.au

Cover design by Independent Ink
Internal design by Independent Ink
Typeset in 12.5/17 pt Adobe Garamond Pro by Post Pre-press Group, Brisbane
Cover image: by the author

ISBN 978-0-6454243-2-4 (paperback)
ISBN 978-0-6454243-3-1 (epub)

Disclaimer:
Any information in the book is purely the opinion of the author based on personal experience and should not be taken as business or legal advice. All material is provided for educational purposes only. We recommend to always seek the advice of a qualified professional before making any decision regarding personal and business needs.

Contents

Introduction

In 1965, a friend gave Shirley and me a book of poems entitled *Prayers*, by Michel Quoist.[1] I still remember the poem about a brick. The poet tells of watching a brick wall being built and focuses his reflection on the importance of each brick being in right relationship to all the others. The poet concludes that we each need to stand in the right place in life regardless of where that will be. Much later on in years I learned how important it was in building a brick wall to place the foundation row of bricks well and in alignment. If the bottom line of bricks is not aligned, the entire wall will be weakened. The foundation is important. It is interesting to note that the foundation row of bricks is covered over once the wall is complete. Those bricks are essential to the wall, but we do not see them. The image from the poem and the image of the brick wall together remind me of the function of our principles. Our personal principles are like that foundation row of bricks, we may not see them but they impact our lives everyday, and place us in appropriate relationships with others. We stand in the right place.

We live in an age of uncertainty. This is not unusual; it seems an abiding truth for us at any time. What seems different now is that formerly dependable institutions, paradigms and narratives seem less reliable and relevant as we seek to stand in the right place. Prowling at the edges of our consciousness are provocative questions: What about me? How do I maintain a sense of being grounded and secure in complex and uncertain times? What about us? In a global landscape, what do I think of others, all others with whom I share this "island home?" What is my purpose? In the short time I am here, what contribution will I make for the common good? What is my right place?

When I first decided to write these reflections about my eight personal principles that help me sustain nonviolent living, I thought it would be an easy task. I am surprised sometimes at how naïve I can be. The more I have reflected on these principles, the more complex the task has become. While this is so, these reflections have been rich with memory and meaning.

Principles are basic tenets, essential and primary truths. They are, for me, like fundamental "doctrines" that govern and guide my life. My principles have a sense of being like bedrock, something solid and unchanging beneath the ever-changing nature of daily living. An image I remember from a book title many years ago is that of the still point in a turning world. The principles are like that still point; a foundation that is steady, emerging from an unchanging, deep, timeless realm of life that anchors me.

In reflecting on how I got here, to these present principles, I realise that the answer is not simple. The question, "How did I get here?" could imply some straightforward linear pattern of development that can be traced with a bit of effort. When I look over my shoulder, I see what one writer described as a bramble-covered stone path that twists and turns over itself time and again. I may be able to see only one or two stones of the path most of the time. Sometimes my life path looks like an interesting and complex collection of experiences that I cannot possibly sort out. It is a life path that does twist and turn, circle back and move forward. Change is the essential character of my life journey. In the Prologue to his memoirs, *Memories, Dreams, Reflections*, Carl Jung affirms that we cannot possibly understand our lives in some final way. He says, "At bottom we never know how it has all come about."[2]

What am I looking for? As life moves and changes, and it does, I am concerned here with the foundation that represents the *unchanging*, those principles that hold steady, that together manifest the still point in this changing world, the anchor for my ever-changing life. Change may well be the one experience we can rely on in life, but my sense of things is that change rests on a deep, core foundation of the unchanging. For me, the principles are just this, this is their function, to hold life steady, to provide solid grounding, to be the anchor as life unfolds. They are meant to be the foundation of truths that I then apply to an endless variety of circumstances, events and relationships as my ever-changing life continues along. They speak of the changeless, the timeless truths; they give a context, meaning and energy to the applications of these truths in daily living. In undertaking the original work of giving shape to these eight principles, what I have hoped for is a solid unchanging foundation. These are the bedrock principles that will govern and guide me in sustaining a nonviolent way of life on an ever-changing life landscape. The principles hold steady, the application of them to life changes, even daily.

The dynamic interplay between the ever-changing and the unchanging has raised two matters for me on which to reflect. First, it invites me to think again of the relationship between "then" and "now," and of the integrity of past experiences. In a conversation with a friend I realised that it is far too easy to dismiss past experiences on the basis of my present understanding; "now" can devalue "then." I remember a line in a hymn from my youth: "Time makes ancient good uncouth."[3] While I realise that the application of my basic principles is continually changing, I want to honour that what I hold to "now" need not denigrate what I held to "then." My present position on any matter may well have in some way grown out of my convictions or opinions "then." The evolution of our consciousness involves ongoing changes and adaptations if we will be disciplined in our self-reflection. To change forward does not require us to dismiss or devalue our past efforts or understandings, even when we are pleased and relieved to move on from them.

As I have gained some clarity around the unchanging principles at the centre of my life, I also understand more clearly now how I adapt these in my living. Two references on application come to mind. The first is from Paul in the Biblical writings. "When I was a child, I spoke like a child, I thought like a child, I reasoned like a child; when I became an adult I put an end to childish ways."[4] Having declared the change, Paul goes on to affirm that, for him, three principles abide. They are faith, hope and love. We learn, we grow, we more forward, standing securely in our basic principles. These hold steady as our application of them changes.

The second reference is from *How to Develop Your Thinking Ability*,[5] by Kenneth S. Keyes, Jr. Keyes reminds us to put a date on our points of view. It seems to me that to put a date on attitudes and actions is to respect their integrity in their own time, and to honour the fact that change alters how we apply our deepest convictions, our principles, to life. It is possible that even the language of the principles may come in for revision as life unfolds.

Second, there is another reflection on the dynamic between the unchanging and the ever-changing that is important. In his reflections on metaphors for peace work, my colleague, Wilhelm Verwoerd, in South Africa, offers metaphors of the garden to balance the metaphors of the brick and the building.[6] In nonviolent living and peace work the two metaphors work well together. The peacebuilding metaphor can help us identify a structural foundation, the unchanging principles, on which our lives and work stands. This metaphor also risks a certain pre-determined inflexibility, building by a pre-set plan, design or process. The garden metaphor offers a variety of more flexible and organic images that spring from working the soil. Our aspirations, our practices, our peace work, as in the garden, are like sowing seeds and planting seedlings. Sustaining our aspirations and efforts for nonviolence and peace requires focused and disciplined attention to what plants we have set out in our own souls and in our shared lives with others. We water and we fertilise to sustain and enrich the buds of new ideas and surprises in growth, and we cultivate the surrounding soil of collaboration with nourishing possibilities in our reflections and interactions. We pull out the weeds and prune when necessary, and accept the fact that some efforts fail, while others succeed. It is the ongoing, changing and organic process of the work that rests on the unchanging foundation of our deepest convictions, our principles. The foundation row of bricks and the garden images are complementary metaphors that intertwine the unchanging and the ever-changing that enrich our understanding of our experiences. In seeking to live nonviolent lives and to work for peace, we both build boldly and cultivate carefully the way of peace and nonviolence.

Can we get to that still point, can we drop deeply enough beneath our changing daily lives into the realm of the timeless in order to identify that first row of bricks? Over time I believe we can. When I was in my mid 20s I heard a very revered and honoured old bishop speak to a gathering. At the time he was close to 100, and died a few years later at 102. His simple message was that love is the core for a meaningful life. This was his singular, enduring principle distilled out of many decades of experiences. I remember sitting listening to him speak and being somewhat awed. It all seemed so simple. Really? Distilled from his experiences, the principle seemed simple, yet the application remains complex. My hope for myself is that these principles capture something of the deeper, enduring truths that have shaped my living over a longer period of time. They function as a bridge between my unchanging foundation and my ever-changing life.

How did I get here? My intention in sharing these reflections is to invite, to inspire and to provoke readers to address the title question for themselves and thereby come to stand more firmly and consciously on their own unique ground for the benefit of us all. Like the bramble covered path that twists and turns over itself again and again, I will touch time and again on the same or similar themes as I make my way through these reflections. I also recognise that this journey through these principles will not give full attention to all issues facing me, and all of us. At best I have shared highlights of the adventure; it is an unfinished work, as am I. If these reflections provoke questions, objections and brooding thought, this will be enough and for the common good.

My principles for nonviolent living

The divine spirit is the life energy of all that is:
all life is interconnected.

At the heart of all life is mystery:
there are many truths I do not know.

My call is to live my life in this larger spirit-life and mystery:
wholeness, not perfection, is my hope.

All creation is my family:
I was born into community.

My inner work shapes my outer life:
what I do not engage within I project onto others.

The way of the cross is the journey to wholeness:
it is the path of love.

Loving is the most important human action:
forgiving is at the core of nonviolent living.

Justpeace is my ongoing hope:
mercy tempers the passion of justice.

14 May, 2010
revised, 30 April, 2020

.

CHAPTER ONE

The divine spirit is the life energy of all that is: All life is interconnected.

Three weeks after Shirley and I were married, I had an assignment due which required me to trace the development of the understanding of God in the Jewish sacred texts that are part of the biblical collection. Evidently I did it well, because I scored a very high mark. We decided that married life agreed with me!

As successful as I was in studying these set historical texts, I do not seem to be able to do the same for myself. The influences in my life are numberless over decades, and unlike historical texts, they are not neatly recorded, and various points of view overlap and interweave with each other. The image that comes to mind when reflecting is of a tangled ball of yarn with which a kitten has had a good play. Looking back, life appears like a tumble of experiences and influences. I also find memory at times only partly reliable.

I cannot now describe what I believed about God as a boy or as an adolescent. I am sure it was a traditional belief shaped by my faith community and involved a personal father God image revealed as part of the Jesus story. My limited world of childhood would have given me little cause to consider differing points of view. At the age of fifteen I was introduced to the psychology of Carl Jung through personal therapy. This framework has had a deep influence on my understanding of God and the stories of my faith tradition. Dream work in therapy opened me up to the vibrant reality of the symbolic life, and this included coming slowly to accept that the God symbols of my faith tradition were windows into something deeper and beyond simple literal descriptions. The value of the symbolic life and the integrity of myth came early to me.

At age eighteen I had an experience that deepened my sense of awareness of God. One evening a friend and I engaged in prolonged conversation about our growing questions of faith. Late into the evening, we decided to go to the church to pray. This was in the days when churches were still left unlocked. As we began to talk and pray, another friend entered suddenly in a state of agitation and frustration. His wedding day was approaching and there were some tensions and differences of opinion among family members about the details of the day. His issues became the focus of our prayers, and in the midst of this time, I became aware of a vibrant sense of Presence, an intimate presence that I could only name as the spirit of God. It was deeply moving, and became for me an enduring, ongoing experience that has continued since that night. While at the time I would have named this as God's spirit, the experience also began to shape an understanding of divinity as a vibrant energy behind and beyond all the specific images of my faith tradition. It was beyond my capacity to define this clearly. I can only say that the Presence felt intimate, and seemed to hold me in positive regard. I find it difficult to express how deeply this experience affected me and how much it has remained with me as a defining sense of the divine life. The descriptive language has changed, but the sense of presence has not.

Some years later I encountered a small book by an American Quaker, Thomas Kelly, entitled *A Testament of Devotion*. The first chapter includes a paragraph that spoke deeply to me of that earlier experience, and the paragraph continues with me as a companion in my devotional practice. This brief passage acts as a summary of my understanding of the energy we call God. It begins thus: "Deep within us all there is an amazing inner sanctuary of the soul, a holy place, a Divine Center, a speaking Voice, to which we may continuously return. Eternity is at our hearts pressing upon our time-torn lives, warming us with intimations of an astounding destiny, calling us home unto Itself.[7] This is, for me, the Intimate Presence.

In *The Varieties of Religious Experience*, William James writes about the "MORE,"[8] and it was certainly that. From my present vantage point I see it as a presence that first was connected to the depths of me, yet separate from my consciousness, and over time this sense of the presence enlarged my frame of connection to include others who are different, then all of humanity, and then all of creation. From my late teenage years, the interplay between my personal spiritual experiences of the Presence, the spirited practice of dream work, and the encounter with the academic study of religions, all began to work together to open my boundaries and horizons. The Intimate Presence became the energy that gives life to all that is. I am inclined these days to use the phrase "Radical Inclusivity" that helps me understand this divine energy. The sense of the all-inclusive nature of this divine energy functions as a foundation for the ethical frame of my life.

Throughout my life the influence of Jung's point of view has continued to play an important role in my understanding. In these latter years I have concluded that Jung's psychological work became my first intellectual framework through the therapy and the dream work, and his work became the lens through which I interpreted the stories of my faith tradition. I concluded long ago that without this symbolic, mythological frame through which to consider the stories and claims of my People, I would not have found adequate nourishment in the tradition. A more literal, historical take on the Christ stories does not speak deeply to me.

Jung's notion of the collective unconscious as a vibrant reality known to all humanity through countless specific and local cultural images and symbols – the archetypes – made increasing sense to me in those early years and has continued to fascinate and excite me. One semester at university I took an elective in California Native American culture. In one instance we looked at a myth common to a particular group of people that paralleled closely a myth of the Greek tradition. There was no chance of outer contact and I was deeply impressed with the notion that these myths seem to arise from what Jung named as the collective unconscious. We were/are all being influenced by a common life source, energy, Spirit.

In 1977 I was introduced to the practice of active imagination as a way of responding to, and working directly with, dream images. In 1979 I engaged a series of active imagination meditations that began with a significant and upsetting dream. The central image in the dream was a Great Dane dog. Through active imagination the Dog, who I named "Dog," became my guide deep into the underworld of my own soul where I met a variety of strange and wonderful people. I undertook eighteen dialogue meditations over two years, and in one of the last experiences I went deeper than ever before down a series of stairs until I came to an abyss. Christ escorted me there. The image of the abyss was vibrant, pulsing with life and was named no-thing. The form of the abyss was vague except that there was a dome shaped top with open tubes that flowed upward. These tubes were the particular ways in which the energy of the "One" flowed into the particular experiences of our outer lives. Here is an excerpt from dialogue sixteen.[9]

> "It was all so quiet and yet so very alive, vibrant. Life pulsed there. Christ told me to be still here – to simply contemplate the centre. He spoke of it as the centre where all is One. Here there is Oneness; as it moves up it is particularised, concretised and appears in forms of good, bad, evil and the like, but at its deepest levels, the Centre – Life is One. Then he walked into the abyss and disappeared saying he'd be back. I sat alone sensing the vibrancy of the One Centre. It was so still, yet so very dynamic. It is awesome, yet also difficult to contemplate."

The experience continued to give more conscious shape to what has become this first principle. *The divine spirit is the life energy of all that is.* Some years later, when researching lists of principles from various sources to share with participants in a workshop, I found a list of principles attributed to Gandhi.[10] The first of these is simply, "All is one." I found Gandhi's simple assertion very encouraging. It resonates deeply with my meditative experience of the abyss where life is One.

In her work, *Listening to the Rhino*,[11] Janet Dallett expands the notion of Spirit. She connects the common origin of the words breath, wind, inspiration and breath of a god, to the word spirit. Using Jung's work with her own, she asserts that at the deeper, primordial levels of human experience, the animating Spirit is One. Spirit is Spirit and it is our responsibility to choose how we

one ...

world
water
air
land
creation
community
village
family

one...

relate to this dynamic Spirit both as a projection outward from us into our common life, and as an enlivening energy within us. This point of view implies a very positive view of humanity, and raises ongoing questions about choice, both the reality of our capacity to choose and our responsibility to choose well. The ongoing challenge is to become conscious of our ability to choose and to make responsible choices for our own good and for the good of all humanity, indeed for the good of all creation. How will I access and express the vital and vibrant divine spirit for the common good? What is my conscious intention?

To affirm the life source for all creation as One, the divine Spirit in countless variations, creates a natural bridge to the notion that *all life is interconnected*. There are countless references that affirm the truth that all life draws from the common source. In a collection of writings by Jung on nature, Meredith Sabini quotes a passage from Jung with a similar image in which he refers to life as being like a single tissue "in which all things live through or by means of each other."[12] The poet Mary Oliver, in a collection of essays, adds her contribution to the notion of interconnectedness in the form of a question: "Do you think there is anything not attached by its unbreakable cord to everything else?"[13] In another essay in the same collection, Oliver states: "I would say that there exist a thousand unbreakable links between each of us and everything else, and that our dignity and our chances are one." Robert Kunzig, in an essay in *National Geographic* magazine, quotes French sociologist Edgar Morin commenting on an important lesson from the Covid-19 pandemic: "The first terrible revelation of this unprecedented crisis is that all the things that seemed separate are inseparable."[14] Barack Obama, through his conversations in his early days as a community organizer in Chicago, comments on how he "came to trust the common thread that existed between people."[15]

This interconnectedness extends beyond humanity to all of creation. I remember learning that trees produce oxygen and absorb carbon dioxide, and this places us in a very direct collaborative relationship. At a conference years ago a woman suggested that once we referred to the trees as you or thou, rather than it, our sense of connectedness would be deeply changed. Photographer, filmmaker, and conservationist Adrian Steirn[16] asserts: "What we do to the animals we do to ourselves." This direct assertion cuts deeper through my defences to affirm that when we harm the environment we damage ourselves. Increasingly I have been challenged over years to become conscious of the amazing interdependence with all of life on the planet. The world in which I grew up either seems not to have understood this, or at least did not share it with me in any significant way. In secondary school I did take a botany class and we grew vegetables at the back of the school property, but issues of environmental responsibility were not addressed. The acceptance of our oneness with all creation has now become a top priority for our survival. *All life is interconnected.*

The truth of our interconnected oneness could become sentimental and trivialised as a romantic notion, but in fact it confronts us with the serious challenge of living daily in a larger frame and for the common good. Am I prepared to live daily in the larger context that includes others, and to realise how my decisions daily have an impact on our shared life on what some have called our island home?

A major issue in focussing on the common good is the reality of difference. Throughout our history different groups among us have taken differing points of view on a vast variety of matters, sometimes fuelled by different opinions of divinity. Our collective history, our shared human story, is scarred with the conflicts we have experienced to try to settle these differences. Conflicts arising from differences continue to be manifest in our local and global lives whenever diverse peoples assert their points of view over those of others. We are still too much in conflict and at "war" of one kind or another.

The reality of our interconnectedness challenges us, requires us, to develop an all-encompassing capacity for diversity in order to protect our emerging life together on our planet. A question I have used on a poster asks: "How much diversity am I willing to tolerate, endure, accept, welcome, encourage, embrace and celebrate?" How much can I handle? It is a core question and a serious concern on a daily basis. The capacity for diversity and respect for differences is another of the critical challenges of our time. Our survival as a global community depends on us finding ways to engage difference creatively and with respect.

The concern for difference raises a whole host of issues. While I may want to stand with an all-encompassing capacity for diversity, in fact I have my *limits*. There is much I do not understand and this will inevitably touch into my fears that run beneath the surface of my attempts to live in this awesome and mysterious world. I aspire to radical inclusivity, but this aspiration does not free me from the anxieties and fears I experience as I encounter the complexities of daily life and behaviours, attitudes, opinions and policies that differ from mine and that I see as destructive to a humane life for us all, and a healthy life for the planet. My aspiration also does not override my knee-jerk reaction to make negative judgements of those who differ from me, and from my points of view. How do I hold my personal limits within the larger frame of radical inclusivity?

It seems to me that the *context* of any issue is core to my assessment of any matter, and this assessment, or discernment, is a never-ending task. The questions whirl around for me. When do I comply with the limits and boundaries that have held me safe thus far, and when do I step out and transgress them in favour of a new point of view? When do I support the policies of my various cultures and government, and when do I take a stand for a different point of view? In his book, *Swamplands of the Soul*, James Hollis take this opposition to dominant culture to a more dramatic level in identifying the myth of the Holy Criminal.[17] When do I support, when do I transgress? In the context of radical inclusivity, how is it possible to stand for a different point of view, to stand in opposition to others and their convictions, and at a deeper level also honour our oneness as the human community?

In some instances the issues of differences/diversity get sorted easily. We quite naturally create small groups or local communities that exclude without judgement those who don't have the requisite skills needed. We know quite well that, as they form, special interest communities need not diminish those not included. Exclusion on the basis of specific talents and gifts is usually a simple matter to resolve. Distinctions of character, gender, skin colours, ethnic groups or sexual orientations take us into more complex areas of life where the ethic of radical inclusivity requires us to reflect more deeply on how to sustain our oneness while pursuing individual interests.

Acceptance of diversity is critical to a nonviolent way of life. What is my response when I experience differing points of view with others that I conclude are degrading and dehumanising of other people, or that are destructive to our global home? My instinctive reaction can be to be intimidated and overwhelmed by the question, yet that does not excuse me from confrontation with it. Over time I have come to realise that it is essential to engage my discomfort with the question, and with the complex issues facing us at every level of creation and human interaction. Joanna Macy, in her image of the Spiral of the Work that Reconnects,[18] offers us a pattern for our encounter. I find this a useful model through which to identify my place in the complex and diverse collective life. I begin first with a sense of gratitude; this is my grounding for a creative response. Out of my encounter with this model I have been writing a daily gratitude list for several years. It keeps me aware every morning of the blessings of the previous day. I then open myself to feel as best I can some of the pain of the world as manifest in the issues before us. For me, this means sometimes feeling a bit overwhelmed and intimidated. It also means feeling connected to some degree with the hurts, rejections, and insults that others feel in the violent transactions between peoples. Thoughtful reflection shared with others on what we see and experience can lead me to look more deeply and with more hope at what concerns us. This then enables me to begin to form a creative and useful response. Once I acknowledge my feelings, I am able to choose a response. Exercising choice consciously is the key element. We come back to context as I consider my response. What actually am I able to do in specific instances given the shape of my own life? The question comes up time and again as part of my ongoing concern for the planet, for others and for myself.

This leads me to reflect again on the issue of diversity *intra-psychically*. How am I getting on with the various aspects of myself? This focus of concern comes up over and over again: How am I with me? Given my lived experience, I affirm that I am the starting place for my intentions and my capacity to sustain nonviolent living. This includes my capacity to engage the diverse aspects of my own self that I picture as an inner village of varied and sometimes conflicted, yet very interesting, aspects of me. I hold firmly to the idea that my capacity to live a nonviolent life depends directly on my capacity to live at peace with me. If I cannot love and embrace myself, how can I possibly offer you my care and compassion? Again we come to radical inclusivity, this time in the context of me loving me.

My temperament is such that I prefer things tidy and in order. My colleague, Alan Jones, once remarked in a presentation: "human life is messy."[19] In reference to differences this is the reality; the conversation is never finished. My encounter with diversity is contextual, daily and endless, ranging from the landscape of my soul, to the landscapes of my neighbourhood and community, to my nation, to the world. That poster again poses the question: How much diversity am I willing to tolerate, endure, accept, welcome, encourage, embrace and celebrate?

In the context of the diversity among religions, Rabbi Jonathan Sacks in *The Dignity of Difference*, presents penetrating questions that can have wider application. "Can we make space for difference? Can we hear the voice of God in a language, a sensibility, a culture not our own? Can we see the presence of God in the face of a stranger?"[20] Engaging diversity is an intra-psychic, internal issue for each of us. It is also an issue among us as groups of people, and more widely an issue in reference to the well being of the planet. The challenge for me is to consider how to engage these many differences in ways that empower and enable me to build bridges and to be radically inclusive. *All life is interconnected.*

If beneath, or behind, our great variety of religious images of divinity and the sacred life, we can catch a glimpse of the animating spirit of all creation that unites us as One, and if we can become aware of our interconnectedness and the oneness of all creation, then we have begun to establish a solid platform from which to live consciously a more nonviolent life. *The divine spirit is the life energy of all that is: all life is interconnected.*

CHAPTER TWO

At the heart of all life is mystery:
There are many truths I do not know.

An interesting starting place for these reflections is a statement by Henry Miller that I found in Janet Dallett's work I mentioned earlier. Miller declares: "Until we accept the fact that life itself is founded in mystery, we shall learn nothing."[21] So we begin with mystery stories.

When I was in my older childhood and early adolescent years, my brother, Frank, and I were into reading the Hardy Boys Mysteries. I don't remember now any of the stories, but I have a picture memory of us standing at the city library desk on a Saturday morning checking out our next supply of books. They were great adventures with a bit of danger and the mysteries always were sorted out in time. Much later on I went through a phase of reading the Agatha Christie mysteries and enjoyed following along as things got sorted out. There are mysteries to be solved.

When I was twenty-two and newly married, I experienced sufficient pain in my lower body to seek medical help. It did not take long to receive a diagnosis with a very long name. Several vertebrae in the lumbar region of my spine had not knit completely. I was told it was a condition from birth and not uncommon, and that I needed to manage the condition with exercise and care. The prognosis was open and a future with a wheelchair was mentioned, though not considered probable. No one then, or since, has recommended surgery. I was fitted with a brace that I wore a good deal of the time for about ten years, and have kept up various exercises and physical therapies ever since.

To say I was devastated with this news at twenty-two is to put it mildly. My future seemed uncertain; it was like a cloud hanging over my life. I remember telling my priest in a session that it felt like someone had taken a sledgehammer and smashed it into the lower back of Michelangelo's stunning statue of David. I felt like a young man done down by life.

In the early days as I adjusted to this new sense of myself, my priest recommended that I read the Book of Job from the Biblical writings. He suggested that I might find a good friend there. I did read Job and found his story very helpful. What really annoyed me in the story were the last verses at the end of the book – chapter 42:7 to the end – that seemed like a "happy ever after" ending. It diminished the profound struggle of Job to understand and accept his life. Later in my academic work I took a semester course on the Book of Job and learned that these final verses are considered a later addition to the original text. The Book of Job originally ended with the Whirlwind speeches of God beginning at chapter 38, and ending with Job's final response at chapter 42:5-6.

What did Job receive for all his tedious dialogues with his wife and friends? What did he receive as he shook his fist at the heavens in the face of his tragedies? He received a deeper, even overwhelming experience of God and no answers. This made more sense to my struggling soul. There was no answer.

What emerged from my encounters with the Job story was a question that is an ongoing companion in my life. "How creatively can you live without your answers?" Oddly enough I take great consolation from this question and have pondered it many times.

Out of the encounter with the Job story another issue about questions emerged over time. I believe this comes from Jung's work, but I do not know where. When faced with such a circumstance as mine it is not unusual to ask, "Why did this happen to me?" The question, for which there is rarely a satisfactory answer, risks leaving us in a victim stance toward the events of our lives. It is possible we will get stuck there and will be unable to move forward. The more appropriate question is, "What can this mean for my life?" Here I find that I am invited by life to initiate a response that moves me forward in some way. It also raises the core desire for meaning, and this is the inspiration for me to engage my life by including whatever the circumstances or conditions I face, and to create actively a life. This is what has been important to me in living with my back condition and the ongoing disciplines of exercise, pain management and care. And I still have no answer. There are mysteries, at times painful mysteries, to be endured.

In 1975, Shirley and I had the opportunity to attend a conference on mystery at Grace Cathedral in San Francisco. One of the main speakers was the anthropologist, Dr. Margaret Mead. I remember hearing her talk about various aspects of the God relationship, including the God who is never to be known. I am sure I must have considered this aspect of the relationship many times before, but in this instance it was like hearing it for the first time. God would always be beyond my understanding, beyond my reason and my ability to comprehend. In this moment Dr Mead's expression of this basic truth awakened me in a new way. There are mysteries never to be solved.

In the early 1990s I was asked to give a keynote address for the convention of a Christian denomination. I was asked to address the question, "Where to when the mystery has gone?" I don't now recall the details of what I said, but do remember asserting that the mystery had not gone anywhere. I focused on issues and practices that would help us live within the mystery of divinity. I was told later this provoked much discussion for the duration of the conference. As I write this I remember an encounter over forty years ago with a woman in her 80s who had listened to a dynamic speaker reflect on the experience of the disciples at the event of the Transfiguration as recorded in the Biblical writings.[22] After the event she came to speak quietly to me and commented that the speaker was dazzling, but she whispered, "I didn't agree with a word he said." The speaker asserted that the divine presence was on the mountaintop, and from there the disciples came back into ordinary life. My elderly friend affirmed that the reality of divinity is around us always, it is we who come and go, tune in or tune out. We live in the divine presence, what I came to name as the Intimate Presence. There is mystery in which we live.

At the heart of all life is mystery. Some mysteries we are able to solve, others we find beyond our comprehension, for some we can find no satisfactory answer and we simply must endure them. Woven into the very fabric of the great Mystery that is life, is the impulse, the niggling energy of doubt, fuelled by the energies of wonder and curiosity. Wanting to know is a strong drive in us and has carried us far beyond our own expectations time and time again. We spend a great deal of energy in our outer and inner lives sorting, sifting, investigating, and researching, trying to come up with answers to what were mysteries at the outset. Doubt, wonder and curiosity are like fuel to a lively life. They enable our capacities to grow, develop, expand, and mature. We long to know and so we explore the mysteries.

It is perhaps more true that the inner world, the realm of the soul, is more the domain of the complex and elusive, the world of mystery, where many questions, for all our reflections, remain unanswered. In the Introduction to his book, *Care of the Soul,*[23] Thomas Moore offers very helpful insights into the mystery of soul. Moore asserts that the "human soul is not meant to be understood" or solved like some puzzle of life. Soul is more to be appreciated for its complexity and paradoxes. Soul is to be honoured for its depth and richness. Soul is to be respected for its ability to hold the regrets and the wounds of our lives. Soul is expressed in our loves and our attachments, and often holds the key to understanding and containing our inclinations toward violence. Soul inspires our values, energises our work and passions and sustains us in the ups and downs of our relationships. Soul defies precise definition. Soulful experiences are as ordinary as a good meal or a heart-warming conversation with a friend. Soul experiences are as extraordinary as a memorable dream, a tense conversation that breaks through to resolution, or a flood of tears that ushers us to a deeper and more honest understanding. As elusive and mysterious as it is, soul is what gives us depth, richness, texture and colour, and makes us human.

The language of soul is that of symbol and myth. In our rational culture, myth is often dismissed as being something that is not true. As I came to understand early on, myth may not be fact, but it is true, and myths function to carry truth that cannot otherwise be expressed. As a devoted reader of fiction I read many stories that are not factual, but that are truth telling. I remember a friend once saying that if you want to engage good contemporary theology, read fiction. The parables of Jesus and the mythologies in our varied cultures may contain little that is factual, but they carry great truths that serve our souls well over long periods of time. Symbolic stories by nature remain mysterious to us to some degree; we do not exhaust their meaning and wisdom. It seems possible that the great myths of our collective history are great because they cannot be fully understood, but offer useful insight and guidance at different times and circumstances.

An ongoing experience of myth is through the world of our dreams. As I shared earlier, I picked up the dream trail in my teens and have followed it now for over 60 years. It is my ever-unfolding personal myth, my trail of symbolic stories that continue to guide, encourage, chastise, confront, inspire and enrich my daily conscious living. Coupled with the practice of active imagination, that included the aforementioned Dog series, my life is an ongoing interplay between the facts of my historical, chronological life and the psycho-spiritual truths, images and myths of my interior soul life. Even with this combination of rich resources and experiences, I still remain something of a mystery to myself. I return to Jung's observation from his memoir and quoted from the Prologue, "At bottom we never know how it has all come about." Mystery – sometimes to solve, often to endure, and many times to engage and to appreciate for the richness we receive.

There are many truths I do not know. The one enduring memory I have of constructing these principles more than ten years ago was the sense of relief that came with this brief assertion. I am still not sure why this is so, but it felt a great relief to realise again and affirm that I do not know all there is to know and will never know all. Julia Baird, in her work *Phosphorescence*, in the very useful chapter on doubt, declares: "We need to know how much we do not know."[24] Through years of responding to my education process, and in the context of my professional life, I realise I took upon myself the pressure to know, and to have answers. It is a relief now at times to say simply, "I do not know."

James Hollis, in his book, *Why Good People Do Bad Things,*[25] asserts that in some circumstances to acknowledge that we do not know is a sign of religious insight and psychological awareness. This acknowledgement can open us to a sense of wonder and awe in the face of our universe and of the deep mystery of our own souls. "I do not know" can function as the doorway to a lively faith of deeper exploration into the inner and outer mysteries in which we live.

There is another side to "I do not know." It is that "I do not want to know." In the context of self-understanding it is true for me that there are times when I do not want to know. At times I resist insight and the challenges of integrating new truths. Often a new insight confronts me with the need to change. It brings a sense of responsibility or a challenge to consider how I look upon myself and how I conduct myself in the world. Jung identifies three words that are a useful summary of the pattern of transformation: insight, endurance, action.[26] This pattern is a simple description of the nature of soul work: an insight comes, we endure the challenge and consider the changes we need to make, and we act.

To know, to want to know, to know I can't know, to want not to know, it is a remarkable mix of reactions to the ongoing adventures of my life. In response to the 2020 pandemic that has swept the globe and challenged us in our daily living, the one word that has emerged over and over again is "uncertainty." We do not know where this global phenomenon will take us, we are acutely aware that we do not know what shape the future will take. A character in the story "The River Nemunas," observes that, "The urge to know scrapes against the inability to know."[27] The statement is a "both-and' summary of a life-long tension. It is the ongoing, exciting and frustrating dance between knowing and not knowing. It captures the irritation of the rub between two desires that are not finally resolved.

One positive outcome is possible from our encounter with the mystery of our own lives. As we learn to live with more acceptance and patience with the mystery of our own lives, our uncertainty can lead us to a kind of humility, patience, an empathy and compassion for others who wrestle as they grasp for certainty in the face of mystery. For me, I return again and again to Jung's assertion in his Prologue – we never know how it has all come about. *"At the heart of all life is mystery; there are many truths I do not know."*

CHAPTER THREE

My call is to live my life in this larger spirit-life and mystery: wholeness, not perfection, is my hope.

In the early 1980s I chose to see an older friend as my spiritual director. One afternoon we sat in his garden for our conversation, and I was expressing some thoughts about my own future and the kind of work I felt drawn to do. He listened and then challenged me with the task of being faithful to the vision once it had taken shape. His challenge to me was confronting, as I was not convinced at that point that I could ever become the man I imagined. The next day, motivated by his challenge to be faithful to the vision, I resigned from several activities in which I was involved, but that did not serve this emerging vision. This vision was hinting at, and pointing toward, vocation.

In 1991, while on retreat in Richmond, Virginia, I read Morton Kelsey's book, *Reaching*.[28] In a particular section he explores the relationship of a sense of vocation to various jobs one might undertake over time. On that afternoon I realised that while I had been trained to see my work as my vocation, it had become for me simply a job. It was a job through which a deeper vocation could be expressed, and I realised that my vocation could be expressed through any number of jobs, or no job at all. My vocation had to do with my character, the man I am in my essence, and this essential character gives shape to, and gets expressed in, the fullness of my life. Later that day on that retreat I undertook an active imagination conversation with some wise figures in my inner village, my soul, and from that meditative conversation, fashioned a vocational statement that has guided me ever since. The jobs have changed several times and the statement has not. I have continued for almost 30 years to write this statement in the front of every new journal.

My call is to live my life in this larger spirit-life and mystery. Calling has to do with vocation, the person who I am called to be. I understand that in the language of the Quaker community, the same dynamic of calling is referred to as "being led." James Hollis explains that the Latin, "vocatus"[29] implies not only a calling but also a summons. To what am I called, into what am I being led, to what am I summoned?

The first implication of vocation includes the sense that someone or something is calling, leading me. Who or what is calling me? A core question for me is, "Who's in charge here?" I come back again to the first principle wherein I affirm that there is a larger divine life in which I live, that connects me to all life. It is a divine energy that calls, leads and summons me into my life. Thomas Kelly, the Quaker writer I mentioned earlier, names it as "the speaking voice to which we may continuously return." It is the voice of eternity "calling us home unto itself." My concern for vocation is a sacred concern; it is to respond to the larger, divine life that animates all life.

The second implication of vocation is that there is purpose in my being here, now. John O'Donohue asserts, "There is a providence which brought us here and gave us to each other at this time."[30] I find this deeply challenging to consider in reference to me, and when I extrapolate it out to the human family my mind boggles. How many millions of us can not get to this realisation and its meaning because of the circumstances of our individual lives? If ever there was a call to social justice for humanity, this is it. Potentially, there is purpose in human life, in my life, and I am challenged to sort out what this will be, *in this larger Spirit-life and mystery.* Kelly's speaking voice is for me the Intimate Presence that I experience as quite separate from my consciousness, challenging me with purpose, calling, leading, and summoning me to my life's vocation. As I have stated, at a deep soulful level of Intimate Presence this vocational statement has not changed, but the expression of the vocation has changed as circumstances change in my unfolding life. My vocational statement remains as I wrote it, but I express it in very different ways than I did 30 years ago. It has seen me through several jobs, and at times is expressed completely apart from any paid work.

A friend's experience illustrates the dynamic of changing circumstances and our vocation. Some years ago this young friend came to talk with me during the time he was making a commitment to life in a Christian Religious Order. He felt he was responding to a deep call, an expression of vocation. After the appropriate time and protocols of the Order, he took his life vows and settled into his life in the Community. After several years circumstances began to arise that caused him increasing discomfort and these began to fuel doubts around his sense of vocation. At one point he experienced an insight that changed things dramatically. In conversation one day he realised that the

God who had called him into the Community, could also lead him out of it. He began to understand that his vocation might be different from this life commitment to the Community. Vocation could well be deeper than the role he was living out as a monk. The insight was deeply confronting and yet it had a liberating effect on him. He began to imagine himself outside the Community but still connected to his religious tradition and to a sense of purpose or vocation. He did leave the Community, set up an independent life, and began to listen for that deeper urge that would reveal his unchanging vocational purpose in life. He was led in and led out and driven more deeply into his own soul. For many, such a change would look to be a failure of some sort. If the Divine life can lead us in and out, then we need to see our carefully considered responses to end a former commitment as being faithful to the deeper sense of vocation that resides in our souls. We are called, led or summoned into lives with purpose and meaning. The challenge for me is to stay as close as possible to the Intimate Presence, the speaking voice, and to be faithful to my call, my summons, that into which I am led.

The third implication of vocation has to do with service. In my experience of family and culture as a young man, I was encouraged to be clear about what I wanted to do with my life. Taking control and making my life happen were fundamental to my sense of maturity and success. A sense of calling was at the edge of this concern. Being called, led or summoned turns this around and poses a more soulful question: "What does life, what does the soul want of me?" I have come across various forms of this question in the writings of others, including James Hollis and Parker Palmer. The question nudges me along and brings up the notion of service. "Who or what do I serve, and how?" I am aware of the statement attributed to Jesus in the Biblical book

In Service ...

To What ?

To Whom ?

.... How ?

of Matthew, that no one can serve two masters.[31] In a frame of radical inclusivity, I strive to include "both-and," but there are times when "either/or" is appropriate. My sense of things is that I can have only one Number One. Who or what do I serve?

I come back to the question with all its sacred implications: "Who's in charge here?" *My call is to live my life in this larger Spirit-life and mystery.* It is to understand that my vocation is a response of service to a larger life, regardless of how I give it form and shape in specific circumstances. At times I struggle with the truth that I am utterly immersed in a shared life at this specific time and place, and confronted with the relentless challenge to step up to the daunting task of being me in the midst of us. I am called, led and summoned to live life well for the common good. Life lived just for me is to wander down a dead end street and to miss the point of the astonishing adventure of our shared lives, the common good.

Having been raised in a rational western culture, it is a challenge to remember that *rational consciousness* is not all there is, that *I, me, mine* [32] is not all there is, that *individual* is not all there is, that *"we"* is the fundamental context of *"I"*, that the notion of interconnectedness in my first principle is not some soppy romantic idea, but a hard biting challenge to remember that my entire life is lived out in the context of our lives, of all of us. Another poster I have created states: "There is no them, there's only us." This is true of me as a complex individual, of us in our local worlds, and of all of us in the global family.

In recent years I have become aware through the work of Desmond Tutu of the term, *Ubuntu*,[33] from the Zulu language. It is translated in various ways including: "A person is a person through other people," "I am human because I belong," and "I am because you are." All these affirm our sense of being part of each other, and all of us parts of one whole. I circle around to the first principle again: *All life is interconnected.* It is a confronting truth that is beyond my comprehension.

My vocation is to live out my life *in this larger Spirit-life and mystery.* The mystery of it all challenges me to live with uncertainty. In this past year of the pandemic, Covid-19, uncertainty has been on the lips of many as we wondered where this was taking us. Some call for a return to normal, and just as many assert that there will have to be a new normal. There is no going back, but where are we going? We are living more clearly in the mystery of life. For all my control needs, I do not know for sure what life will look like, if I ever did. The title question, "How did I get here?" has become a somewhat bewildering and amusing question. But here I am, living *in this larger Spirit-life and mystery.*

Wholeness, not perfection is my hope. The core challenge for me is to choose the path guided by the image of wholeness, rather than perfection. There is a significant backstory to this assertion. Many years ago I learned that the English translation of the verse in the Biblical book of Matthew, chapter 5:48, is an inadequate and even misleading translation of the original Greek. The English reads: "Be perfect, therefore, as your heavenly Father is perfect." The word translated perfect is *telios.* The Greek is more accurately translated as complete, whole, full, rounded out. The passage then is meant to challenge the reader to aspire for a whole and complete life, not one that is perfect. My hope is to be whole and complete in my life experience, not to be perfect. I consider this mistranslation of Matthew 5:48 to have had disastrous consequences for Christian spiritual practice.

The starting place for a reflection on wholeness and perfection is that neither is achievable. I have not read anywhere that perfection is considered achievable. Approximate wholeness is the phrase I saw somewhere in Jung's work. Both words, as concepts, act as overall frames for our aspirations to become our best persons. As I have experienced and reflected on these words over time, I have concluded that, as aspirations, perfection tends to exclude and wholeness tends to include. These are very different pathways, and give form and shape to very different spiritual values and practices. In practice it seems that perfection is sought through excluding undesirable aspects of one's self. We seek perfection by getting rid of feelings, thoughts, attitudes that we don't like, that are uncomfortable, and that upset our sense of our ideal self. For years I listened to people exclaim that they need to get rid of their anger, judgement, selfishness, lust and even their very egos … and on goes the list. The spiritual path in this model is a constant battleground with the natural experiences of our emotional lives. In this frame we are constantly working to get rid of something that does not fit the conscious ideal persona, one that is often formed by our various family, faith and cultural influences. Too often we are riddled with guilt at our shameful feelings, or vengeful attitudes, our lack of compassion, and our indifference to our own sufferings and the sufferings of others. I conclude that the path of perfection can only embroil us in endless conflict with ourselves and set us up to condemn others who remind us of the secret selves we don't want to be. During the time I was writing this section I watched a documentary about the lives of a group of men who chose various forms of the Religious life. One of them talked about having to tame his passions and negative thoughts, and to fight diligently against himself in order to achieve his ideal of spiritual maturity. The practice he described was to keep busy and to choose to avoid his own undesirable thoughts. His life sounded like an ongoing battleground. For me this is not a transformative path. From my youth in the therapy context I was encouraged to face up to and accept whatever bubbled up from the unconscious, and to see it as a part of me that must be honoured and accepted, even though it might not be expressed outwardly.

In those early years I was invited to take up the path into wholeness, though this language was not used at that at time. For me, the path of wholeness has become synonymous with the commitment to radical inclusivity. It is a path of transformation. Jung writes in one essay: "We cannot change anything unless we accept it."[34] The transformative path of inclusivity begins with acceptance of whatever is the issue rather than avoidance of it. Terry McBride affirms this process of acceptance: "Our task is to make conscious and embrace all aspects of ourselves (even the most undesirable …)"[35] McBride asserts that to refuse this task of self-acceptance is to contribute to the conflicts and tragedies of human life.

It is simple enough to choose the way of wholeness, the path of radical inclusivity, the practical issue is to identify and enact the practice that supports the choice. How do I live into wholeness, radical inclusivity? While I aspire to an overall framework of wholeness in dealing with myself, with my local world and with the entire global creation, I find that the notions of wholeness and radical inclusivity can be overwhelming on reflection. How can I take in the entire global family and creation? Wholeness, inclusivity and diversity all raise again the blunt truth of my limits. I carry limits that have been set early and deeply in me by culture, family, faith and individual temperament. There are all manner of inner experiences and outer differences that push against my sensibilities, my preferences, my moral guidelines, and my capacity to understand. Coupled with these are the natural limits of humans for relationships.

Recently I have read Matt Haig's novel, *The Midnight Library*, and therein have encountered the notion of Dunbar's number.[36] This idea was new to me and so I searched in Google for more information. In the 1990s Robin Dunbar conducted research work at the University of Oxford on this issue and claimed that we humans are wired in our brains to sustain about 150 relationships in stable societal structures. There are various responses to Dunbar's work on the Internet; my concern here is to recognise that we may well be limited naturally by the scope of our capacity to have some sense of meaningful connection to the global family and the creation. Some years ago I read of a character in one of James Joyce's novel, who repeatedly declared, "Here comes everybody." I still twitch when I imagine everybody coming my way. I will support wholeness and inclusivity globally, nationally, locally and internally, but it is a challenge as to how to put this into practice. I remember a guideline attributed to David Suzuki: "Think globally, act locally." In terms of daily practice this can be useful. Another question emerges. In the context of my daily life and limits, what is actually practical in terms of a practice that is inclusive and supports the aspiration of wholeness? For me this begins with inner work and it includes affirming regularly that the context of my life is ultimately global. This, for me, is the work of the soul, and it is core to my practice for nonviolent living. My practice in my immediate daily life challenges me to affirm that I am interconnected with all who I meet and pass by in my daily moving around. This sense of being interconnected has led me to take seriously acknowledging in some way those I meet as I take my exercise walks and those with whom I share lanes when swimming. My intention is to make others visible and to honour their presence, however fleeting. The challenge is more confronting when I observe others acting outside my approved conventions of behaviour. The challenge extends to those who hold opinions on important issues that are different from mine. I come again to the ongoing issue of difference. Just how much can I tolerate, endure, accept, welcome, encourage, embrace and celebrate? Certainly these issues are global and national, but they are also local, familial and internal. I aspire to wholeness, and it drops me to my knees. Yet, with all its challenges, it is the overall frame I choose. Mystery again, I am confronted with the mystery of my complex inner life, our complex national life and our even more complex global life. The questions linger to provoke my continued reflections. How do I include the diverse, the radically diverse, mystifying, confusing, enraging others, and the differences by which I am confronted? How?

From another point of view, when it comes to my sense of limits, I need to be aware that on the far side of the boundaries I set up for myself there may be treasure hidden. Jung's concept of the Shadow challenges me to realise that there may be gold in what makes me uncomfortable, or in that other "me" I fence off from what is acceptable. A part of dealing with difference, with the diversity of my own life and soul, and our vast differences as a larger family, is to realise that my wholeness and our wellness will at some point include my engaging what is uncomfortable, confusing, unnerving, unbelievable and even distasteful. Mystery. *My call is to live my life in this larger spirit-life and mystery; wholeness, not perfection is my hope*, for me and for us all.

CHAPTER FOUR

All creation is my family: I was born into community.

Where to start here? First, it is in this principle that I have made a word change from the original work. The original statement was, "All humanity is my family …" After ten years I changed it to *All creation is my family …* There are stories.

So, there we sat. We had come around the corner on the dirt track in the truck and there in front of us right at the track edge was a bull elephant who immediately questioned our presence. Karen, my guide and driver, turned off the engine and we sat very quietly while the elephant flapped his ears and stomped his foot a bit. Karen spoke very quietly to him. I remember words like, "It's alright boy, it's okay." He flapped and stirred up dust and we sat. We talked about the tusks, how they were unequal in size and easily weighed about 100 pounds each. One swipe across the cab of the truck could be very serious. So we sat. Finally he seemed to tire of all this and walked away. When he was a safe distance away Karen started the engine and we went on our way back to the house.

It was my last day at Malilangwe Reserve in Zimbabwe. I was there with two young friends and having daily experiences of the animals in their own habitat, and coming to some deeper sense of life together. On that last morning Karen had offered to take me out to look for a black rhino. "We have to find you a black rhino," she said, as we boarded the truck. She knew that the black rhino is very special to me and I was pleased at her offer. On our two hours out we saw many different animals and even spent some time looking at rock paintings that were very exciting for the artist in me. We had no luck finding a rhino, so we headed back to the house for lunch. Along the way we came to a part of the dirt track that was very rough due to rains, so we took a detour around to the left. And then it happened. Karen spotted it first. "Look, over there," she said and sure enough a black rhino came up from a "pan," a mud pool, and came straight for the truck. She came close, made some noises and danced away, then returned and did the same, again coming within metres of the truck. After the fourth approach and dance away, she paused and walked off into the brush. The visit was over. Karen started the engine and we drove on. Karen remarked that she had never seen anything like it. It was then we came around that corner and ran into the bull elephant. What an amazing last drive out into the reserve.

While the notion of the oneness of all creation was quietly moving around in my unconscious for a long time, these experiences in Africa helped bring this to the surface, and subsequently led to the word change in this principle. Somehow the encounters at Malilangwe, and before this at Wild Ark in South Africa, opened my consciousness to a wider picture of the oneness of all creation. I now like to think of the bull elephant as an agitated cousin, and think of the black rhino as a friend.

The rhino has been special to me since my teens and became

even more important because of a dream some few months after Shirley died. I name it now as my totem animal. The members of the staff at Malilangwe were able to identify this black rhino from the ear tags in my photos, so I know my friend as Ganyani, at the time a five-year old black rhino. Her picture hangs on my lounge room wall in a place of honour.

There are other stories of the importance of nature from my childhood and forward. I grew plants alongside the garage in my childhood. At University I would sit on a bench in the spring across from an oak tree to enjoy the new yellow-green leaves coming out. As a boy I enjoyed hiking in the hills with my brother and our friends. As an adult, whenever I went to the monastery in the hills above Santa Barbara, I included a long hike up into "Rattlesnake" canyon as part of my quiet time. Sitting near the stream on a rock and reading a book and eating a sandwich were very soulful times.

During the Covid isolation time in 2020 I read of a study that concluded that 20 minutes a day in nature were good for maintaining mental health. It's true for me. One of the selling points in buying the home in which I presently live, is the large tree on the verge. It provides shade and colour and is well used by the local bird communities. *All creation is my family.* I continue to grow into this affirmation with an expanding awareness as to how to live cooperatively with my Creation Community.

I was born into community. I have touched on the notion of community in several ways, as I go round and round in reflecting on these principles. It comes up again and again in consideration of diversity-differences, inclusivity, the common good and the context of the collective for the individual journey. In this instance I have in mind the core archetype of belonging, one of the deepest desires of the soul.

I have taken the second statement of this principle from the work of John O'Donohue. In his writing, *Eternal Echoes*, he asserts: "We do not make community. We are born into community."[37] When I first read these statements I had a bit of chuckle when I realised how much effort over years I put into making or creating communities. I welcome the truth that, at the broadest and deepest levels of our experience, it simply is a given fact of our existence. Within the Creation Community we form, for better or worse, smaller communities, but the encompassing Community prevails and challenges us. We belong by birth.

An influential image for the one human community comes from *The Book of Forgiving*,[38] by Desmond and Mpho Tutu. In their work the authors affirm that we modern humans come from what scientists call Mitochondrial Eve, our matrilineal ancestor. We are all cousins of one another, at most ten thousand times removed, and we are all Africans in origin. My encounter with this idea was very significant for me as it provided another language map to affirm the truth of being one, in this instance across skin colour and cultural divides that had marked my early years. We belong as cousins.

Wade Davis, in his work, *The Wayfinders*, extends this further using the findings of genetic science. Research confirms that there are no dramatic differences in the genetic endowment of populations across the world. Even the most remote peoples in the world community carry fully 85 percent of our total genetic diversity. Davis concludes that scientists have now confirmed what philosophers have long believed: "We are all literally brothers and sisters. We are all cut from the same genetic cloth."[39] We belong as brothers and sisters.

The implications of our one Creation Community are far reaching. We are invited to build a framework for our living on these truths: we all belong by birth, are all cousins because of our common origin and are genetically brothers and sisters. Thomas Aquinas in the 13th century, penned a poem entitled, "The Mandate."40 The declaration of the poetic reflection is that "Nothing in existence is turned away." In his 13th century world all belonged; "No creature should be turned away." All belong in our one Community.

In her poem "When the Holy Thaws,"41 Teresa of Avila questions the great wars between countries, including "The countries – inside of us." She questions the "insane borders we protect," and declares: "Only at that shrine where all are welcome will God sing loud enough to be heard." In her 16th century world she affirms that beneath or beyond our countries, borders and differences all are welcome, all belong from God's point of view.

In reflecting on the first principle I referred to Adrian Steirn who asserts that: "What we do to the animals we do to ourselves." We cannot hurt the planet without hurting ourselves. *All creation is my family: I was born into Community.*

It is uplifting and inspiring to collect these ideas together and affirm this principle, the challenge is how to live it. I keep coming back to "How?" to action and daily living, and circling round on the same ground. The simple, fundamental stretch for me is to seek to open my mind and heart to the sacred nature of belonging in the largest possible sense. *All life is interconnected.* Keep the global framework in mind when making local, specific and daily decisions. I have hung a photo of the planet earth from space in my entry as a reminder of our shared life. Invest energy in global issues and the well being of the planet. Engage our concerns for the health of the planet, for climate change, for nonviolent processes in addressing differences. Speak the concerns, speak the oneness, and let these become a spoken frame for local living with others. Be daunted by the overwhelming scope of our challenges, then take a deep breath and keep on moving forward in whatever way fits my particular circumstances, limits, gifts and skills.

To affirm that *all creation is my family* is, in a sense, to declare a non-negotiable principle and truth. I am able to negotiate belonging and involvement with various communities, but I can't escape the absolute belonging wrapped up in this affirmation: *"All creation is my family."* In terms of human belonging, I had an insight on the death of my brother in July 2019. We had not spoken for twelve years and had been estranged for many more. The story is sad, and not relevant here. What happened for me when he died is that I felt grief and sadness deeply and was a bit surprised. What has helped me since then is to make a distinction between bonding and relationship. I am now clear with myself that I was bonded to my brother over all those years, but a relationship was something we could not sustain. The relationship is negotiable; the bond is given. It makes sense to me to extend this to the entire creation. By virtue of my existence I am bonded to all creation, this is the given. At the same time my relationship circle is limited and may be very small.

This affirmation of the bond leads me to affirm that my small gestures, for good or ill, are like droplets of influence into the larger common pool of creation's energies and our global wellbeing. It does matter what I say and do in terms of the health and wellbeing of humanity and the entire creation. An ongoing question for me is: What energy do I choose to contribute to the common good? From another point of view, I remember a theologian colleague years ago declaring that there is no private sin. Whatever we do, for good or ill, has influence on the entire human family and creation.

The given nature of my bond to all creation and humanity

raises the dynamic of the interplay between the individual and the collective in endless forms. I find it helpful to think of it as the ongoing dance between self and other, or the individual and the collective life. The interplay between the two requires regular consideration. In his novel, *The Prophets*, Robert Jones, Jr., has one character reflect, "The individual always has to give up something for the group."[42] Do I do *this* for me, or *that* for others? The questions and decisions are part of daily life.

Jung's process of individuation is relevant here. Individuation for Jung is the process of growing into one's unique self through the ongoing dialogue between consciousness and the unconscious. The context for my individuation is our shared life, and an awareness of my responsibility to the common good. It is a process that includes engaging with intention my involvement with all others and the creation. It is vastly different from the life path of the self-serving rugged individual. It is the life task for me, for all of us, to discover and express our unique sense of self, with an eye to contributing this unique life to the common good. Sometimes I opt for my own agenda, other times I give up my way for the common good. There are times when the dance is tense between the two, and at other times the energy flows easily, but it is an ongoing, daily dance. *All creation is my family, I was born into community.* The dance of self and other will come up again with principle six.

CHAPTER FIVE

My inner work shapes my outer life: what I do not engage within I project onto others.

Iremember well two inner events during my tertiary years of study. First, in my first year of study at a community college in California, I took a psychology course, Psych 1A. I remember arriving one morning for my class at 8:00am and sitting in the back of the room. While the lecturer was speaking I was writing down the dream I had the previous night. I was running late that morning and had not had time to write it down at home. The dream is what mattered to me. Second, in my last semester at the university I remember having a "big" dream about a Wagnerian-styled opera performance on campus in the main courtyard in front of the library, and also seeing underground tunnels running up to fraternity row several blocks away. I wrote the dream out in my journal as it made a deep impression on me. When I later explored the dream with help, I became aware of a major theme in my life that had been stirred up in the university setting. It is about the balance of thinking and feeling, and it has remained an ongoing theme throughout my life. I will come back to the subject of dreams later.

My inner work shapes my outer life. Inner work for me centres on the process of self-reflection. My practices are intended to increase my capacity for a growing self-awareness, or consciousness. The over-arching goal of these practices is to enable the sense of increasing wholeness identified in the third principle. It is a process that has no final point of arrival in sight. I do expect to continue to grow into a greater wholeness as life unfolds and as I attend to my life's experiences through self-reflection.

For me, radical inclusivity is a fundamental characteristic of wholeness. Everything that happens in our lives, all our dreams, hopes, catastrophes, feelings, reactions, and thoughts are included. This aspiration of wholeness summons me to a relentlessly honest self-awareness. Over and over again I am challenged to acknowledge my feelings, to claim my experiences and to tell myself the truth. Two well-known statements are attributed to Socrates: "Know thyself," and "The unexamined life is not worth living." A colleague told me of using the latter statement in an assignment in graduate school and getting chided for its harshness. He was asked to remember those many people who do not have the luxury of time or the capacity for self-examination. I would agree that it has a harsh edge to it. Another colleague who practices an eastern religious way told me of a remark made by a teacher in a group session. The teacher asserted that the defining mark of human life is self-reflection, and since many choose not to undertake the rigors of the task, they are leading less than human lives. Again, this sounds a bit harsh. Harsh as both these comments are on the wider landscape, they carry truth for me. These brief story events lead me to do whatever I can to encourage others to engage the tasks of self-reflection and to experience its benefits in shaping their outer lives.

Self-reflection is for me the key; it summons me daily. This is reflected in the title question for these reflections: "How did I get here?" I was pretty pleased in the aftermath of the 2020 American election and its chaos to hear a television journalist pose the question to the camera audience, "How did we get here?" How has this happened? The self-reflective questions are a direct way onto the landscape of my soul, and our reflections have the power to shape and reshape both our inner and outer lives.

How did I get here? I want to acknowledge a broader frame that informs my daily life before I reflect on specific practices of inner work. As I previously mentioned, at the age of fifteen I entered weekly therapy with my parish priest, Morton Kelsey, who had recently studied at the Jung Institute in Zurich, Switzerland. I worked with him most weeks until I moved into Los Angeles to finish my first tertiary degree. On return from university I continued the sessions with Kelsey, during which time Shirley and I were married, and we then put in place our plans to move across the country to Philadelphia where I finished my training and second degree. The result of those five or more years of therapeutic work is that the psychological work of Jung did become my primary intellectual framework, and the Christian story has been interpreted through this lens since my young adult years. In 1997, after many years of not seeing each other, I met with Kelsey in California to discuss my PhD research. In our conversation he self identified as a Christian who used Jung. I realised then that I was primarily oriented to Jung's framework and fit my Christian commitment into that frame. Much of my work over the years has included efforts to broaden my personal frame in order to hold in creative relationship the spiritual practices of my faith tradition and the psychological practices that I have learned in the context of Jung's psychology. I refer to this as a psycho-spiritual framework for living. This is inner work, the disciplined practice of self-reflection. Core to this inner work for me are three ongoing practices, *dream work*, *journal writing* and *active imagination*.

First, working with the *dream*. The brief stories about dreams during my university years demonstrate that, for me, attention to the dreams came early, from age fifteen onwards. As these stories illustrate, the dreams, and the recording of them, were the starting place of inner work. Once I experienced insight from these strange stories, I was committed to listening as best I could. I have been following the dream trail now for over sixty years, and I continue to be amazed at the guidance I receive. The dreams[43] are for me the speaking voice that Thomas Kelly names in the amazing inner sanctuary of the soul. Among the benefits I receive from the dream stories are insights that can be very challenging. I also receive encouragement, confirmation of outer decisions, guidance for future actions, and warnings when I get off track. The stories can be pleasant, confusing, affirming, fascinating, exciting and frightening. Nightmares do come at times, but I have come to understand that even these offer me a useful point of view. The dream stories sometimes are often complex and difficult to understand. The stories bring together people and places that in my outside life were not connected in either time or space. The dreams speak a coded language of symbols, and we in our culture are not well trained to speak this language or to value it. Even after all these years there are times when I am left wondering how to gain some meaning from a story. It has been necessary for me over the years to have people around who will listen with me to the dream stories symbolically, and who can help me gain some insight. Learning to speak the coded symbol language of our dreams takes careful attention over time, and the language is different for each of us. Catalogues of dream symbols that are generically defined are rarely of any use in sorting out the potential value and meaning of my personal symbols. It is worth noting that there are times when I remember only an image from a dream, much like a still photo. There are mornings when the dreams slip away under the pressure of early morning thoughts, and these are among my more frustrating experiences.

On reflection I think what touches me most is that over years, these stories have given me a sense of an unfolding life rich with meaning. I often refer to the dreams as my personal mythology. They speak truth, my truth for the meaning of my life. It is an understatement to say that I am grateful for this long procession of dream stories. When I last saw Morton Kelsey, in 1997, he lamented that he, at his age, no longer remembered his dreams. He said that he missed his dream stories as one would miss long time and valued companions. I felt a deep compassion for him as we talked; whenever I can't recall these night stories I feel a loss of guidance for the day. The richness these stories offer my life is quite beyond description.

In reference to the dreams, there are two brief points I include here. One is in reference to recall. Scientific research has concluded that we dream three to five times a night. When someone tells me that they never dream, I share the research that indicates that we do, and suggest the issue may be one of recall. If we have never been told that our dreams are important, then we do not have any inclination to remember them. There is an exception in this matter of recall. It seems that some medications adversely affect recall of the dreams. For most of us, to recall our dreams is a matter of changing our attitude toward the dream stories and usually our recall will improve.

The other point has to do with control. The dream is clinically referred to as an involuntary psychic product. We do not choose our dreams, nor do we construct them. For me, they are created by that speaking voice, as Kelly names it, that is at the core of our souls, and they come as products from the unconscious that arrive in their own time, a time that is timely for us. My task is to work to decode the symbolic language and gain what insight is offered. Perhaps one reason people shy away from the dream is that the stories are not in our control. In a culture that prizes rational consciousness and control, dreams remind us that we do not control all aspects of our lives. We may control our recall, but the stories are independent of our conscious control, and I believe this is their primary value. Ongoing attention to my dreams is my way to participate in the dialogue between consciousness and the unconscious. It is a dialogue with the speaking voice, a dialogue in which I participate rather than control. Dream work, inner work, challenges me to re-think the degree to which I am in control of my life. In reflecting on vocation in the third principle, a core question that emerged there comes again here: "Who's in charge here?"

Second, *journal writing* as a practice to record my dreams began in those university days. In 1963, during that last semester at university, I remember beginning a new journal by writing a greeting on the first page, "Dear God." Journal writing was my response to the speaking voice that came through the dreams. It was and has remained my primary way to participate in the dialogue. The journal content now includes the dreams, any active imagination dialogues, and reflections on any incident in my life that stirs emotional responses. I also have used the journal to plan programs and presentations, and more than once have actually made presentations directly from the journal pages.

Journal writing came easily for me. I attribute this to the discipline my mother set up for us in our childhood. When I was five, my mother initiated a separation and divorce from my father and took my brother and me from New York City to a suburb near Los Angeles to be near my aunt and her family. One practice on which my mother was very firm was that we had to write a letter to our father regularly. They were very simple letters and this went on for some years through primary school. I still remember the beginning: "Dear Daddy, How are you? I am fine." I do not know when we stopped these letters, but what I conclude is that I developed the habit of writing in those early years and this transferred easily to journal writing later in my teens when I began the adventure of therapy. In my younger adult years I wrote less regularly, and sometimes did not write for months at a time. I am not sure now when journal writing became a daily discipline, it has been too long ago to recall. What I do know is that journal writing became, and is, one of the core practices of my inner work. In recent years I have used A4 visual art diaries of 60 pages, and tend to fill about four per year. I keep them for about a year and sometimes review past entries, but then destroy them. Some friends have suggested that I keep them to be shared, and that is not going to happen! My journals are written for me and as a part of the dialogue with the divine energy that is largely centred in the dreams and reflections. I find that the journal is a valuable place to reflect with myself and to practice as much honesty as I can manage. I think it's fair to say that most of us do not intend to publish what we write in our journals.

Third, my inner work reflections were greatly enriched with the added experience of *active imagination*. As I mentioned in the reflection on the first principle, in 1977 my analyst, Weyler Greene, introduced me to this meditative practice. I had presented a dream that was troubling and he suggested that I try to speak with the key dream figure, a Great Dane dog. It turned out to be a very helpful dialogue, and I have continued to use the practice to engage significant figures. My PhD research work[44] focused on comparing the experience of active imagination with Christian religious experience, using my own experience along with the experiences of four other participants.

Active imagination is a meditative process of entering into dialogue with dream figures or other significant images in an attempt to listen more deeply to the diverse and complex voices that are naturally a part of us. It is as a result of this work over the years that I have adopted the image of a village as the "place" to contain all these various inner people, or sub-personalities, who have emerged over the last several decades. The village provides a safe and friendly container in which I can encounter and honour the various different aspects of me, and learn to listen at times to their different points of view on any current and pressing subject. A long time colleague of mine came to value his villagers so highly that he developed the practice of consulting with his key villagers whenever he had a significant decision to make. Once we engage ourselves in this model, we discover just how rich, varied and wildly diverse we are. This inner work dialogue with the unconscious is a key practice of the individuation process as described by Jung.

The inner work practices of dream work and active imagination raise another important issue. I indicated earlier that it is my opinion that we are trained in our cultures, often in our families, and even in our faith traditions, to direct our lives from our rational and conscious point of view. Both these practices challenge us to re-consider the value and importance of the active contribution of the unconscious to our daily lives. A result of this work for me has been to shift the imagined centre of my life from an ego-centred consciousness to a mid-point between consciousness and the unconscious. For me, the meeting ground of the mid-point is the village with all its interesting and diverse characters. Like my friend, I consider it unwise to make any important decision until I have listened to the contributions of the unconscious through dreams or in active imagination dialogues. The "holy place, a divine center, a speaking voice," of which Kelly speaks, is a sacred source of wisdom that speaks our truth, often inviting us beyond the conventional and established wisdom of our present conscious point of view. It is a serious challenge to re-centre our living from the narrow boundaries of a rational monologue into an open-ended dialogue with the symbolic images and stories of our souls. Listening to these truth-speaking ones from within also begins to build a firm foundation for the inner authority that we each need for a more complete self-realisation on the path into wholeness.

These three aspects of inner work, journal writing, listening to my dreams and engaging in active imagination dialogues, are basic for me. The goal of this work is wholeness, and the practical result of our efforts is to help ground us in that still point in a turning world. I also like to think of the work as anchoring me solidly in a foundation that shapes my outer life and strengthens me to engage the chaos, surprises and storms of everyday life internally, locally and globally. For me this anchor is the Intimate Presence.

I find it helpful to imagine that these three practices of inner work are held in the wider frame of *soulful living*. I am not sure how else to say this. First, inner work is not just drudging work, but often is a great pleasure, and it brings deep satisfaction and meaning. It is challenging, requires discipline and is a great joy. The larger frame of soulful living for me has been made more clear from reading Thomas Moore's *Care of the Soul* which I mentioned in the second principle. The land of the soul is an elusive and imprecise landscape. I am wandering here on an interior landscape that refuses order and simple clarity. Soulful living can require discipline and careful planning, but is also a rich and nourishing landscape that includes spontaneous, simple and unexpected pleasures. Often soulful living involves an endless variety of ideas, opinions, attitudes, experiences and even conflicting points of view. Soulful living offers satisfactions at our accomplishments, joys in moments of meaning, and an agitated curiosity about the "more" that lies ahead.

As I see it, what is soulful for me is highly individual. We each need to identify and honour those soulful moments and qualities that enrich life. It's interesting to note how different these soulful experiences can be for us. Each of us has the freedom and responsibility to create the soulful framework that assists us in being grounded in the still point and anchored in the deep life energy, the Intimate Presence.

Before writing this section of my reflection, I spent considerable time over several days reflecting on the common qualities that lie beneath our widely varied, individual and specific experiences. What, for me, creates a soulful experience? Some descriptions that stay with me are: having time alone, engaging in silence or quiet, gazing out into the largeness of nature, and gazing into the mystery of my own being, musing, brooding, wondering, being attentive to the moment and whatever it is that has caught my attention, unhurried, a leisurely pace, being present to an occasion and to others, a sense of effortless connection to others, being held in a larger presence or spirit of the moment, a sense of giving myself to the experience or occasion, and losing awareness of time. Where does this list stop?

Likewise a listing of events, moments, and activities will run off the page. For me, enduring soulful living includes: times of prayer and devotions using resources from various faith traditions, taking time to remember others in need, brooding in my journal over a dream or other insights, spending time in the garden or in a park walking, listening to birds, watching the clouds form and reform, listening to music, sharing in vulnerable and thoughtful conversations with others, making time to read in quiet, engaging my collage art work, swimming my laps at the pool and often engaging others there in conversation, thoughtfully preparing my food and tidying up, and allowing myself to feel pain, anxiety and compassion for others, including the wider communities of the planet. And on it goes … More than specific moments or events, soulful living has to do with an overall attitude for life. It involves openness, curiosity, expectancy, interest in life as it unfolds and a reverence for whatever is at hand. It is to want and to work for what is best for others and for me. Inner work and soulful living *shape my outer life.* They help me be a person of some quality for others as well as enriching my life journey.

What I do not engage within I project onto others. The second part of this principle reminds me of the critical importance of this inner work. What I will not engage, what I avoid or push away, often gets pushed onto others. As Terry McBride[45] asserts, this is "… the source of all the woes that beset humankind." It was in that Psych 1A class I mentioned earlier that I learned about negative projection.

How quickly I seem inclined to project my unfinished inner business onto others. Two American theologians put forward one-liners that have stuck with me. Richard Rohr says in more than one place that what is not transformed is transferred. What we do not transform through our inner work sneaks its way out in the form of a negative projection onto others. Walter Wink reminds us that what is pushed away does not go away. Whatever it is that I deny or refuse to face will simply sink back into the unconscious and wait for another opportunity to surface, usually in the form of a negative projection onto someone else.

It seems it is common practice for most of us to project our unfinished business onto others and see them in a negative way. I concluded long ago that I am able to assess easily what is going on for me by the enemies I keep. My sense of things is that this is true for others as well. To project those parts of us we deny onto others is a form of violence. Negative projections are dehumanizing of others. In the year 2020, in the chaos of the American election process, the negative projections flew wildly across the country. It is not surprising that the post-election tensions erupted into actual violence. The challenge of nonviolence, practiced through our inner work, is to give up the luxury of enemies. In the Biblical book of Matthew, the teaching of Jesus goes further as he challenges us to love our enemies.[46]

In the Jungian model we are here engaging the concept of the Shadow.[47] It is the other side of us that we often do not know, do not want to know, deny, avoid and project onto others. Whenever I am uncomfortable with another person, whenever I find another person's attitude or behaviour disturbing, off putting or disgusting, I am on the threshold of "Shadowland." From my point of view, I consider Jung's ideas about the Shadow one of most important contributions he makes to our self-understanding both in our inner work and in our relationships with others. If I am to sustain my commitment to nonviolence and a nonviolent way of life, I need to work to know myself as fully as possible, and to work to withdraw or withhold my negative projections, and address my negative responses as part of my inner work.

None of this is new to us. I have found it helpful to realise that the Shadow concept as put forward by Jung has roots in ancient insight. I would guess it has been with us for as long as we have been conscious. In reading James Hollis' work on the Shadow, I encountered a statement attributed to Terence, a Roman poet. I did a Google search and found a Wikipedia source. Terence, Publius Terentius Afer, from Tunisia, was an African Roman playwright during the Roman Republic. His comedies were performed for the first time around 170–160 BC. His relevant observation is: "I am a human being, I consider nothing that is human alien to me."[48] From the second century BC we can move forward to the 12th century AD to Francis of Assisi. In a poem attributed to him he asks: "Can true humility and compassion exist in our words and eyes unless we know we too are capable of any act?"[49] In the novel, *The Breaking of Eggs*,[50] a man searches for his mother after the Second World War. He is too late to find her, but finds a long letter that she left for him in the hope that he would come one day. In it his mother tells him a painful story from her own life experience in the war years. In the telling she explains: "But one of the reasons for telling you this whole story, if you don't know already, is to impress on you that there are no limits to what any human being may do in certain circumstances." The experience of the Shadow has been with us for a long time. If we do not do our inner Shadow work, we risk continuing negative personal interactions and supporting social structures of violence.

Inner work involves honest self-reflection, practicing emotional honesty, and engaging, even suffering, the truth of myself as much as I am able. Peace, nonviolence, compassion and empathy

COMPASSION:

TO SUFFER WITH

IF I WILL EMBRACE THE SUFFERING
ME

I MAY BE ABLE TO EMBRACE
THE SUFFERING
YOU

begin with my attitudes toward me. In an encounter recorded in the Biblical book of Luke, Jesus challenges the person who questions him to love "your neighbour as yourself."[51] I remember my priest in my teenaged years commenting that this is precisely the problem, we love others as little as we love ourselves. The capacity for compassion has its genesis in our capacity to love ourselves, all of us. Once again the overarching challenge for me is radical inclusivity. One of my art posters reads: "If I can embrace the suffering me, I may be able to embrace the suffering you." This is the core truth of compassionate, nonviolent living.

While we usually meet the Shadow in negative forms of projection as we undertake our inner work, it is also true that there is a golden dimension to our Shadows. This is that realm of hidden dreams and creative desires, and of aspirations to express talents and gifts that did not seem practical in earlier years. The golden Shadow contains that deep wisdom and truth that we may be afraid to acknowledge and express, or that we have been encouraged to revere in others. Tucked away in the nooks and crannies of the golden land may well be deep desires to take up a new career path or a form of artistic expression, to undertake a journey into experiences once thought unthinkable, to serve others with no thought of return, to be recklessly generous with our resources and time, to engage an unexpected and unusual relationship, and to spend time supporting people who are doing it tough. The possibilities of our hidden golden dreams and desires are endless. The Shadow often contains the very energies and attitudes that will promote our wholeness if we can find ways to listen to and acknowledge this mysterious Other.

It interests me to ponder that we might strengthen the bonds of our human solidarity for the common good by acknowledging that most, and maybe all of us, struggle with Shadow issues.

What might we be like with others if we could shift our attention away from the present cultural tendency to over-moralise our negative Shadow experiences, and explore instead what might be the meaning of our negative projections? What might these experiences teach us? What might we, each of us and together, look like if we encouraged our expressions of the gold hidden within the nooks and crannies of Shadowland? If I get stuck in a negative judgement of myself in the face of negative Shadow experiences, I may miss opportunities to engage deeper insights that will contribute to my wholeness and my compassion for others.

Some years ago I heard a Jungian analyst who was from another country, speak at a local gathering. The one remark he made that has stuck with me is that withdrawing projections is a life-long task. This form of inner work does not go away or get resolved. It remains as part of our ongoing commitment to a nonviolent way of life. It is, therefore, a crucial ethical task and a transformative spiritual practice. It is also consistently hard work and disciplined inner work. Various writers have put forward the truth that consciousness, self-awareness, is the key to sustaining this chosen life. As the teacher in the eastern way stated to his students, self-awareness is the essential characteristic of a human life.

There are two quotes that fit here for me and that tend to rattle me when I read them. The first is from Nelson Mandela. I found it in a collection of his letters[52] put together by friends in an attempt to show a more personal side of this man. I was very excited to find this collection and looked forward to reading it. On the first page, in the very first sentence, I found this: "I shall stick to our vow: never, never under any circumstances, to say anything unbecoming of the other …" What a way to start! This is very confronting. Is this possible? What am I to do with the Shadow?

The call is to persistent and disciplined inner work. Reaching back in time to the 14th century I read a similar line in a poem by the Sufi mystic, Hafiz.[53] The poem is entitled "I have come into the world to see this."The line reads: "… men so true to love they would rather die before speaking an unkind word …"Again, is this possible? Through what refining fiery furnace must I pass to even aspire to such vows, much less live up to them? Can I be so captured by love that I am able to acknowledge and contain the negative Shadow and risk expressing its golden qualities? Is it possible to withdraw my negative projections, to undertake my inner work and even to risk engaging my golden dreams, in order to live with compassion for myself, and share this with others for the common good? This, it seems to me, is the challenge. *My inner work shapes my outer life: what I do not engage within I project onto others.*

CHAPTER SIX

The way of the cross is the journey to wholeness: It is the path of love

As I reflect on this principle I remember three events. Some years ago I passed through a very difficult time and was quite shaken. I spoke with a friend who told me he would ring me every day over the coming week so that we could talk. He wanted to make sure I was okay and to support me as I adjusted to my challenging circumstances. I still remember his kindness. A few days after we held the memorial service for my wife, Shirley, a client rang and asked if he could take me out for afternoon tea. I decided to accept his kind offer. We soon thereafter ended the therapy relationship and found ourselves growing into a deep friendship that continues to this day. At one point while we still lived in the same city, we shared most Monday evenings together. These usually involved prowling a favourite bookstore and having dessert and a cuppa. Also after Shirley's service, another friend rang and asked if he could pick me up to go out for a while for a wander and lunch. This happened several times during the early months of my being alone and I looked forward to whatever he planned for us. All three of these men were busy with their own lives, but they made time to look after me when things were very difficult. I am still deeply touched as I remember and record their kindnesses.

The way of the cross is the journey to wholeness: it is the path of love. The focus of this principle is the crucifixion of Jesus as recounted in the Biblical writings. It is a cornerstone of my faith tradition and deeply personal to me. As a young man carrying my share of troubles, I remember going through a period when in times of meditation I would imagine sitting on the ground and leaning back against the foot of the cross on which Jesus was hanging. It was a very safe place for me. I have worn crosses of one design or another since my teen years; to this day I do not remove the one I presently wear except if required in medical circumstances. Crosses of various styles hung in our homes over many years. In moving to a smaller home it was a pleasure to give some of those crosses to friends along with a story of their origins. I still have the small one I made of wood at 18 and used to wear. I deeply appreciate the crucifix from Africa in the traditional abstracted style of African art, and the standing cross from the Ethiopian Coptic tradition, both of which are in my lounge room. The cross matters to me.

What does the cross mean to me? What is the way of the cross for me now? As a young boy and then man I would have subscribed to the proclamation that Jesus died for my sins. This is the substitutionary theory of the atonement. Jesus did for me what I could not do for myself. Over years of education and learning, and with the influence of Jung's thinking in his writings, I have moved to a different point of view. I no longer find the substitutionary theory of the atonement to hold much meaning for me. I now look upon the crucifixion as a model for transformative spirited living. To say it another way, the crucifixion is not something Jesus did for me, in place of me, to appease God. The crucifixion now stands as a loving action that shows me how and what to do. I must do my own work of the cross. We are challenged to take up our cross and to follow in the Jesus way.

The way of the cross is the journey to wholeness. I define the crucifixion of Jesus simply as *a voluntary act of sacrifice in love*. This is my understanding of the cross, and this frames how I am to use the way of the cross as a pattern for my living. I am summoned to voluntary acts of sacrifice made in love. Wade Davis, in his work, *The Wayfinders*, highlights the fact that the word sacrifice is based on the Latin, 'to make sacred'.[54] I am on sacred ground here as I seek to understand how to engage the way of the cross as a pattern for living. As in the stories of the Jesus tradition, the character of our actions includes sacrifice in love, healing, liberation and transformation. Whatever we make of the historical crucifixion, for me it acts as a pattern of how we are to cooperate with the divine life for our healing, liberation and transformation, and likewise for the healing, liberation and transformation of others.

Looking through the lens of Jung's work, the way of the cross is an archetypal pattern, and it is manifest in endless experiences, and many cultures. Over time I have developed three ways of looking at this archetypal pattern as it contributes to the journey to wholeness. These three ways overlap and are interwoven with each other, yet each expresses a somewhat different dimension of this way.

The date was 28 March 1973. After many years of reflecting, avoiding the issue and getting close to facing it squarely, I finally caved in and admitted to myself that I could not control my alcohol consumption; I was an alcoholic. I had spent the five previous nights testing myself to see if I could stop with one drink, and I failed every night. The next morning I took the children to pre-school and drove home crying. Through tears I admitted to Shirley what I finally acknowledged to myself, and the journey of sobriety began. Life was such that I could not make time for AA meetings, so I enlisted a friend who was in AA to connect daily with me for a time. A second friend joined us and the two of them became my AA meetings. The one lasting memory I have from the early days after the decision is of me lying on the bed one afternoon and realising that if I lived to age 81, I would have to survive for 50 years without alcohol. I was overwhelmed. As I write this I have just marked the 48th year of my sobriety, so… almost there, one day at a time. Of all the decisions and accomplishments of my life, this choice to surrender and choose sobriety is the one of which I am most proud and for which I am most grateful.

I use this story to illustrate the first way I apply the crucifixion model, the way of the cross, to my life. The death of an attitude or practice as I share here represents the first step in what we define as the death and resurrection cycle, seen in the death and resurrection of Jesus. Whatever the historical facts and details of those events, the archetypal, symbolic truth played out on the cross teaches me it is possible that our choices of spiritual or psychological death can lead to a new experience of life. *A voluntary act of sacrifice in love* leads to life. The willingness to die in some way to an old behaviour or attitude, an out-dated opinion or thoughtless practice that is often of no value or even destructive, can lead to a new way of being, a resurrection. As in the Jesus example there can be much humiliation and pain associated with this dying, there can be a time of silence like being in the grave, but the movement in the archetypal pattern is forward. The energy in the cycle can shift from the pain and stillness of death to the joy of new life. In the Biblical book of John there is a teaching attributed to Jesus about a seed dying. It reads: "Unless a grain of wheat falls into the earth and dies, it remains just a single grain; but if it dies, it bears much fruit."[55] In my lived experience there was a surprising upsurge of energy for life in the weeks following my decision for sobriety. I did feel like a new person, even if there were times I felt a bit shaky. All the energy I used supporting denial was unleashed into life in a positive way. I realised I was liberated from a lie, I was not in control of my alcohol consumption.

In this first pattern there needs to be a clear decision for death. What in us needs to die? We need to name that to which we have clung that now no longer serves us. We submit to the pain of surrender, we remain steady in the still, silent death-like moments, and if we will hold on and stay with our decision to change, the new attitude, the new vision, the new way forward can emerge. The death and resurrection cycle as seen in the death and resurrection of Jesus is a remarkably ordinary and useful pattern that can guide us through our own times of significant transformation.

The second model that helps me make use of the crucifixion pattern comes from the work of Jung. In Volume 18 of the *Collected Works* there is a lengthy section of questions and answers under the title, "Jung and Religious Belief."[56] The section is a record of written correspondence between Jung and two men. It is in this correspondence that I find another way to make use of the crucifixion, the way of the cross. Jung asserts that Christ was crucified upon the opposites of his own destiny. Through his crucifixion Christ does not offer us an escape from our tasks, but shows us a way to take up our tasks in our own time and to be crucified on the opposites of our own destinies. For me this has both personal and social implications. The notion of the opposites is essential to our understanding of this point of view. For Jung the energies of the psyche exist in pairs of opposites just as they are often observed in nature. For him, the psyche is nature. In this specific instance, Jung is concerned that we acknowledge the unconscious Shadow as the opposite of our conscious perspective on life, and to work to hold these opposites in a creative tension that can ultimately lead to an entirely new understanding. It is for this we work with great effort, to hold the opposites in conscious creative tension. It is in the midst of this tension that we make our considered decisions, and out of our choices a third thing, or a new way, may arise that can honour both aspects of the whole.

Jung asserts that in the symbolic realm, Jesus' crucifixion was on the opposites of his destiny. His task was to embody both human life and the divine energy. This he did over time in love, and withstood the forces of systemic evil that could not overcome the forces of love. The third thing that arises is the resurrected one, the one who engages evil in love and prevails. Evil is not annihilated rather it is fully engaged, taken in, contained and transformed. In Jung's correspondence he focuses on the wider, collective implications of this task for humanity. Humanity is challenged to engage the collective Shadow or risk facing ruin as a global family. The way of the cross here challenges us collectively to the same task in our time. "Othering," scapegoating, blaming, employing violence to feel safe, will not work. We are summoned to engage those with whom we disagree and work to see if we can find a new way forward that is life giving for us all in our diversity. In his time Jung declared, "We cannot talk the H-bomb or Communism out of the world. We are in the soup that is going to be cooked for us, whether we claim to have invented it or not."[57]

On the personal level this second model of the way of the cross offers us a way of engaging ourselves that helps us move toward a greater wholeness. The pattern challenges us to hold together the opposites of our being, to live with the tension of "both-and," with such fidelity and perseverance that a third thing, or new perspective, often can arise from the tension. Robert Johnson takes this further in his reflection on the dynamic interplay of the opposites in our lives. He uses the image of the burning bush from the Biblical book of Exodus, chapter 3. He points out that in the story the bush will not burn and the fire will not go out. Neither bush nor fire will give way to the other, the dynamic tension of opposites holds. Johnson tells us that whenever we have this experience, God is present. He names this as the conflict-without-resolution which was for Moses, and is for us, a direct experience of God.[58]

So here there is death but with a different emphasis. This model for me has direct application to choices I make daily to pursue one path or another in the context of life. In the short term of the day I may well set one opportunity aside in favour of another, but in the longer term view of my life I recognise that I am holding opportunities that sometimes represent different ways forward and may even be in conflict with each other. The way of the cross in this instance is more about carrying our complex selves as we make choices in daily living. More than once in supervision my supervisor and I have chuckled over the truth that the harder choice is often the better one. These choices can be *voluntary acts of sacrifice in love* in which I surrender to a considered reflection through which a deeper and wiser decision can emerge. Transformation here does not come by choosing what must die, but navigating through our options and choosing sometimes *this* path, sometimes *that* path. In a sense what dies here is our tendency to choose prematurely one way over the other. The death is to the either/or paradigm and a rising up to a new understanding of the both-and way of living. What often rises up is a very different and more inclusive and loving attitude toward ourselves and a more creative way of navigating our complex lives.

How do I experience this crucifixion of the opposites within me, this way of the cross? In the fourth principle I used the example of the dynamic tension between self and other in reference to community. It is an ongoing and sometimes crucifying challenge to balance our attention to self and attention to others. Recently one person named it as the tension between service to others and self care. Balancing introversion and extraversion for me is another way to think about this same challenge, and it seems a common and daily experience for anyone in significant relationships.

In terms of contending with the opposites inwardly, many complementary pairs of my character emerge as I reflect. I can be generous-selfish, confident-uncertain, adventuresome-cautious, trusting-protective, enabling-overpowering, strong-weak, courageous-afraid, needy-contained, liberal-conservative and on goes the list. For me a common pair is to live with the dynamic tension between the desire to be active and the need to rest. I am still learning appropriate pacing as I balance my enthusiasm for action and my need to stop and take a break. The task here is to hold the complementary opposites in dynamic relationship, to see potential value in each and to let them influence each other. It is to honour both of any pair and to see that they each will give appropriate influence in specific circumstances. It is to function in the both-and model to work for wholeness. This is not a matter of balance in a 50-50 sense of things, but a realisation that the balance shifts on the scale in circumstances as they arise. For me this way of the cross involves choosing between my desires and options for my own betterment, my wholeness, and for the common good regardless of the cost.

I am concerned that we have lost the transformative nature of these examples of the way of the cross in the claims of doctrines and dogmas. Both of these patterns, the death and resurrection cycle and holding the tension of the opposites, are common everyday experiences as we live with ourselves and with each other. Both are intra-psychic, and both influence our relationships. Both potentially are patterns of transformation toward our wholeness, if we will endure suffering our complex selves.

There is a third symbolic pattern of transformation that we find in the crucifixion, the way of the cross. American theologian Gary Commins highlights this in a reflection. He states that it is deeply challenging to "embrace the idea that our own risks and sacrifices can redeem others, restore peace and revolutionize society."[59] This brought to mind a teaching I received in my church youth group as a teenager. The assistant priest in our parish, affirmed that we are able to make an intentional sacrifice for the good of someone else. It need not be very dramatic or complicated. The core of the action is our intention. This, as an act of faith, is also the fundamental truth at the heart of intercessory prayer. We are able to release positive energy toward another for that person's benefit through a conscious, *voluntary act of sacrifice made in love.* This act of faith also rests on the first principle: *all life is interconnected.* Marcus Borg, in *The Heart of Christianity,* identifies the four-fold foundation on which this faith rests.[60] This foundation of our faith is our intellectual assent, our trust in our lived experience and that which has grown out of it, our fidelity, our loyalty to our faith proposition, and our vision of life that springs from this faith.

This pattern of transformation from the crucifixion, the way of the cross, continues to challenge me. I was raised in that 20ᵗʰ century ideal of the individual who made it on his own efforts. To be interconnected is a challenge enough, but here I am summoned to realise that my intentional sacrifices, no matter how ordinary, when made consciously as an act of love, can bring blessings to others, even if I do not see the benefit. In a conversation with Gary recently we affirmed that, in this frame, every action matters. We are interconnected with each other and all creation, and simple gestures can have far-reaching effects. This is the soul-searing truth of this pattern from the crucifixion, the way of the cross.

By way of summary, I identify three intertwined models for living the way of the cross that I draw from the crucifixion of Jesus. The first way for me involves a decision for a death that is quite clear and sharp, and requires me to live through the pain of my decision. The ego conscious point of view here gives way to a deeper wisdom. In my example this involved giving up the deluded sense of being able to control my alcohol intake and of always being in control. I was not and could not be in control, and the clear decision for abstention, for sobriety, was the way forward.

The second way involves a decision to navigate between opposite possibilities. It is living in an immediate sense of daily small resolutions, and in a larger, longer frame of no resolution, that challenges my ego consciousness to navigate, now this way, now that. Here it is a matter of carrying the tension in the long term. There can be daily decisions, navigations, between opposite options, demands and requirements, but there is no final resolution. If there is a death in this way of the cross, perhaps it is the death of our desire for a simple, either/or life. We make our way among and between complex choices day by day. The examples that keep coming to mind are those daily choices between self and other. Do I do something for you or spend the time doing something for me? Do I serve the other or practice self-care? The choices I make today may not be the choices for tomorrow. I live with short-term resolutions, and no resolution in the longer term.

The third way is an act of faith in which I choose to believe that my sacrifices, at times very simple gestures, can be of benefit to others and add to the common good. These sacrifices are very varied, including my monies, my prayers or my time, but the intention is to benefit others.

These are three experiential ways of the cross that are different and overlapping and that are *voluntary sacrifices made in love*, and contribute to our own healing and transformation and to that of others.

At the beginning of this reflection I shared three simple gestures that three friends made to me: daily telephone calls as I faced a very difficult time, being invited out for a cuppa, and being treated to several outings and lunches in the midst of my grief after Shirley's death. These were simple, voluntary sacrifices of time and energy made in love by others for me. More than ten years on I am still touched by the memories of them, and I know that these have had a lasting impact on my desire to pay it forward.

As with the first two, this third pattern of the way of the cross is a common and ordinary experience in life. The three overlapping patterns share the same challenge for me. The three summon me to step out of my present ego-conscious point of view, to step again into a larger life frame and risk a new idea or effort or action. In his work on male initiation, *Adam's Return*, Richard Rohr declares: "Life is not about you, but you are about life."[61] The crucifixion of Jesus invites me into a larger frame of life and gives a sense of depth and sacred meaning to the most ordinary actions both inner and outer. The crucifixion of Jesus as an archetype of death and resurrection functions as a foundation for transformational change and is as common as can be. I find that my interactions with others take on a deeper and more sacred meaning when I use the way of the cross as the larger frame in which I live.

Many years ago I was involved in a conference that was aimed at helping lay people in a parish explore opportunities for ministry. The facilitator took an entirely unexpected direction in suggesting that what really was needed was a different way of looking at what people were already doing in their daily lives. She reminded participants that the Red Sea had already been parted, and that what we needed were "new eyes with which to see." This became the conference title. I find myself wanting to anchor the way of the cross in the same way. We make sacrifice daily in myriad forms and use these various patterns without much thought. Perhaps what is really needed is to re-frame what we are doing in the larger, sacred frame of the way of the cross, *the voluntary sacrifice made in love*. This way of the cross is *the path of love*, and this brings us to the next principle.

CHAPTER SEVEN

Loving is the most important human action: Forgiving is at the core of nonviolent living

I was nineteen and had enrolled in a state college in Los Angeles for my last two years of university work. Shortly before the semester began a friend rang to tell me that there was a full tuition scholarship in my field up for grabs at the University of Southern California. I followed up on the information, applied for it, and was awarded the scholarship. I got myself into action mode and secured a room in a boarding house off campus and made plans to move there. I had one concern; I owed people money. I had been a little loose with a new credit card and I had bills to pay. I approached Morton Kelsey, my priest and therapist, with a simple plan to solve my problem. I asked him to pay off my debts and I would then organise a payment plan with him when I found part time work at the university. He said no. I was shocked and hurt and felt unsupported at the outset of this great opportunity. No, that's what he said. He then offered another plan. He encouraged me to write to each of those to whom I owed money and explain my opportunity, and to offer to pay them back in small amounts once settled at university. He offered to back me if any refused my request. So I wrote and all accepted what I asked. I then organised to pay each of them back at $3.00 a month during my first year at USC. What did I learn? I learned the life-long skill to budget money and to discipline my spending. Later I came to understand that Morton's decision was an act of love. The first phrase of this principle is an adaptation of a sentence from Kelsey's book, *Reaching*, that I read on that retreat in Richmond, Virginia, in 1991, and referred to under principle three in reference to vocation. He writes: "The first step in loving is making a decision that love is the most important human action."[62]

What is the loving thing to do? In 1966 I attended a weekend event with Joseph Fletcher in New York City. Fletcher's work was in situation ethics, that is, that the right and good decision we make must always be in the context of the situation. In the days of absolute morals and values that were applied across all circumstances, he was controversial. He made a substantial impact on me, and much of what he offered from his perspective shaped my moral and ethical points of view. From the conference emerged the question that I still ask myself when sorting out an opinion or action: What is the loving thing to do? In any given situation, how do we determine the path of love?

I have long felt we struggle with loving because we have this one word that covers an immense territory of relationships. In my world the word was contaminated with Hollywood cinema overtones that made it even harder to sort out how to love. Somewhere long ago in my studies I learned that there are three words for love in the Greek we encounter in the Biblical writings. They are *eros, philia* and *agape*. Eros and philia refer to loves that are most often mutual, sensual, embodied, and include a significant sense of warmth. While these two are usually intertwined with agape in our experience, agape also has a very different character. In my faith tradition, agape is the term used to describe the love that God has for humanity. It is non-reciprocal, that is, it does not depend on a response. There is no pay back in this, rather the notion of "pay it forward' is the appropriate response. Agape is an act of the will and does not depend on an emotional or sentimental content. The essential intention of agape is to want the highest possible good for the other. It is noteworthy that agape is the Greek term used in Biblical book of Matthew, 5:44, cited earlier in the fifth principle, wherein Jesus challenges his hearers to love their enemies. It does not mean to become friends or best mates, it challenges us to work for the highest possible good for the other, any "other." It is an act of the will. It is a form of love that motivates us to act for the good not only for our loved ones, friends and neighbours, but also for strangers, people in crisis and even for those we see as enemies. This love can take countless forms depending on our circumstances. Physically I'm not able to participate in demonstrations or protests, but I have come to see that, my donations to social justice programs serving people in crisis and need represent agape love. This is one way I can work for the highest good of others.

For me, these three forms of love are intertwined in most of our relationships. I am challenged to realise also that they represent a wholesome way to love myself. For me this means to take my body seriously, and to attend with care and compassion to my physical needs, to befriend with respect the whole of me as best I know me, and to be disciplined in enacting that which makes it possible for me to live out my highest good. The question from the conference in New York City all those years ago remains an ongoing benchmark: "What is the loving thing to do?" This loving includes how I love myself and then how this enables me to be a loving person with others.

When I read Robert Johnson's memoir, *Balancing Heaven and Earth*, I came across the fact that the Sanskrit language has ninety-six words for love.[63] This opened up the field of loving to a much wider soulscape. I was quite surprised and curious enough to go to Google. I typed in "ninety-six words for love," and found numerous sources, one of which offers the ninety-six words in Sanskrit. While I am not taking up Sanskrit, I found myself feeling liberated in loving. Our English word carries a heavy burden to express ninety-six different ways to love. Since reading this in Johnson's book, I have reflected on how awkward it seems to acknowledge our various loves except in familiar and somewhat narrow and established social relationships. My sense of loving others has opened up with this insight and I find my sense of connection to others flows more freely, and with greater concern and commitment. For me, in the midst of all the opportunities to love others, the question remains the benchmark: In any particular situation what is the loving thing to do? The question helps me focus my concerns, intentions and energies as I engage others in the context of this *most important human action*.

In my reading in recent years I have found three quotes that I find helpful in focusing on love as my most important action. The first is from the 8th century Islamic/Sufi poet Rabia. In the poem, "The Way the Forest Shelters," she asks: "How will you ever find peace unless you yield to love?"[64] How indeed? Whatever else love requires it challenges us to yield, to surrender to an impulse greater than our ego conscious point of view. I take a great risk when I yield to love. Hafiz, also from the Islamic/Sufi tradition in the 14th century, ends his wonderful poem, "I Know the Way You

Sanskrit has ninety-six words for love

wOrds for lOve

English has Only one

Can Get," with this exclamation: "All a sane man can ever care about is giving Love!"[65] Hafiz invites me to understand that my most sane moments are when I take the risk to yield to love. My sanity depends on how willing I am to love.

Julian Barnes begins his novel, *The Only Story*, with this provocative question: "Would you rather love the more, and suffer the more; or love the less and suffer the less? That is, I think, finally, the only real question."[66] The stories of the characters challenge me to ponder the more painful aspects of loving another toward the highest good. If I yield to love I must embrace the suffering that often comes from loving deeply. My sanity depends on it.

What is the loving thing to do? My reflections on my lived experience lead me to want to write this question on my heart with permanent ink. To love, to express agape intertwined with eros and philia, to love in any of the ninety-six ways, is to be willing to surrender to suffering at times. It is through this mysterious and sane way of loving that we move toward our wholeness, and support others seeking to do the same. This takes us back again to the way of the cross: to make voluntary sacrifice in love. *Loving is the most important human action.*

Forgiving is at the core of nonviolent living. "Just let it go … just … let it go." How many times have I thought or heard this? My friend Bob used to erupt with frustration when he mentioned this line. He heard it from time to time in Twelve Step circles. "How the hell do you do that?" he would ask. We agreed that most of the time it was an attempt to avoid whatever the issue was at the time. Another favourite glib response of avoidance for me is, "Never mind." My response to this is to "put a smile on your denial."

My lived experience leads me to assert that what is pushed

away does not go away. The feeling or attitude I reject, or the wounded one hidden away in my inner village I try to ignore, simply slips back into the unconscious and waits for another time to emerge. It seems to me that denial simply contributes to an ongoing internal civil war.

How do we forgive? How? I am not sure I have ever really understood what such a process looks like. There have been times when I felt something was resolved and forgiven, or let go, but it is not very clear as to how it happened. The most helpful resource I have encountered is *The Book of Forgiving*,[67] composed around their own experiences by Desmond and Mpho Tutu. I referred to it briefly under the fourth principle. For me, this book is a resource of biblical importance. As I compose these reflections, the work of the Tutu's is very much a contributing frame for my thinking, for how I got here.

As I reflect on the "how" of forgiveness, I envision three aspects to the experience that are overlapping and intertwined. The three are: forgiving myself, forgiving others and being forgiven by others. I do not want to set out some tidy, linear process, a kind of step one, step two plan for resolution. It seems to me that forgiving is a more complex, murky process that will vary in terms of intensity and character. This said, I do think there are certain qualities of the experience that inform all three aspects of forgiving. In the fifth principle I affirm that *my inner work shapes my outer life*. Forgiveness in any instance requires disciplined reflection, hard inner work.

The starting place is forgiving myself. If I cannot forgive myself, I will find it next to impossible to forgive anyone else or to accept forgiveness from others. In the novel *The Clockmaker's Daughter*, the character Lucy shares the following observation with Leonard: "I have lived a long time and I have learned that one must forgive oneself the past or else the journey into the future becomes unbearable."[68]

Out of my experience it seems to me that the first step in forgiving myself is to acknowledge and accept that there is something to forgive. This may be an action, and it may also be an opinion or attitude that I hold within myself. Often it is about me failing to measure up to my own ideals, or to fall well short of my aspirations. It may be me violating myself just as much as me violating others.

To work toward self-forgiveness begins with telling myself the truth regardless of how difficult or humiliating this may be. I need to tell the story to myself; it starts here. For me, journal writing provides the most familiar way to stop, to become quiet and focused, and to write out the truth of whatever is the concern or issue. A part of the writing exercise is to reflect as best I am able on how this all came about. What has caused me to take on this opinion, attitude or action? What has motivated me to act in this way toward myself or toward another? Basically I am exploring the question that is my title here: how did I get here? Part of this reflection is to set aside my assumed righteousness or superiority and get down on the level playing field with all humanity. Affirming our shared humanity is basic to forgiving. In the first principle I affirm that *all life is interconnected.* There is a sense that the work of self-forgiving is a way to align myself again with humanity. Part of this reflection also invites me to revisit both my aspirations and my expectations. As important as these are, they can sometimes get in the way of my being an ordinary human being, just one of us. I cannot count how many times I heard my mother sigh and say, "There but for the grace of God, go I."

This forgiving work often requires a visit to Shadowland. In forgiving myself for having violated myself I often have to face up to Shadow attitudes toward me in which I expect too much or too little of myself. I have carried in my Shadow fears, expectations and values from my culture, family and faith traditions that have not always served me well. From these three sources of influence I have also thought ill, or acted badly, toward others. I am painfully aware that I have taken on unconsciously many negative projections over the years that I have had to carefully deconstruct consciously. The poet Terence reminds me that if a human being can do it, I can do it, whatever "it" is, and there have been times when I have burdened others with my unconscious Shadow.

Those who have experienced some version of auricular, or private confession will remember that after the listing of sins, the penitent proposes amendment of life, that is, the penitent intends to change. Here is a pivotal moment; it is the choice, the decision to work for change. Choice is a core element in any process of forgiveness. Self-reflection as part of self-forgiving includes our conscious decision to change our way of acting, and to revise our opinions and attitudes concerning ourselves and others. This, for me, is the hard work, and without it I cannot sustain self-forgiveness. The implication here is that any occasion for self-forgiveness is an opportunity to understand more fully who I am, and to clarify how I want to be in the world.

Written into the very fabric of self-forgiving is the need to make a choice, a decision to face forward into a new way of being. As Lucy says to Leonard in the novel mentioned, part of this process of self-forgiving involves accepting that I cannot change the past and that it cannot be denied or rewritten. Whether I have violated myself or harmed another person, I must choose to accept the fact that I cannot rewrite my past story. My "what if" and "if only" reflections are dead end streets. To accept the past and to make peace with things as they were, enables me, invites me, and challenges me to begin to look forward, and to choose how life can be different for me.

Forgiving myself is a complex, sometimes confusing process and will differ according to circumstance. Certain elements seem essential: to acknowledge and accept the issue, to speak truth to myself, to reflect with care, and to choose consciously different responses and actions that move me forward in my journey into wholeness.

There is another factor here that for me is crucial. I do not encounter self-forgiveness alone. Essential to this healing experience is the love of others who know the secrets and failings of my story and character, and who still love and value me. We come again to the notion of Ubuntu of which the Tutu's speak, the notion of community. Ubuntu: "A person is a person through other people, I am because you are, I am human because I belong."[69] My wife Shirley grew up in Hawai'i where the sense of community was very strong. As a child everyone was Auntie and Uncle to her. She once commented that she was in her later childhood years before she realised that she was not blood related to all these "family" members. The saying, "it takes a village to raise a child," was for her a life long theme. It seems to me that it applies to us all and for all of our lives. As part of this sense of Ubuntu enables us to be ourselves, it is also often true that others have faith in us until we are able to believe in ourselves. When I chose sobriety I struggled to feel positively toward myself for some time, and was not confident that I would be successful. I leaned heavily on Shirley's confidence in me, until I felt able to embrace and believe in myself in the face of my challenge. My aspirations toward wholeness happen in community. No one is a "self made person."

To forgive myself often involves critiquing my expectations, reviewing my aspirations, making my way out from under the tyrannies of perfection and purity, or the delusion of superiority, and realising again that it is okay to be an ordinary, and uniquely gifted human being. It is more than okay, it is the only real option, and a remarkable one at that. Through my inner work of self-reflection, acknowledgement, truth telling and the acceptance of the fullness of my humanity, I have come to experience that it is possible to be reconciled to myself, and to experience over time a deep sense of being at home in the complexity of myself.

While we are able to work for reconciliation with ourselves, it is important to realise that reconciliation is not always possible when we have wronged or hurt others. We sometimes are left to sort out a process of self-forgiveness, and identify our learning for the future, without being able to rebuild a bridge with another. I have known such instances and I can only hope that in forgiving myself I have been able to affirm a shared humanity with those I have injured and hold them in quiet compassion and positive regard.

How do I forgive others who have wronged or injured me? In my faith tradition we identify from the Biblical texts seven statements Jesus makes as he is dying on the cross. We refer to these as the Seven Last Words of Christ.[70] The statement that is traditionally listed first is: "Father, forgive them for they do not know what they are doing." In the well known parable entitled the Prodigal Son[71] from the Biblical book of Luke, we read that the son "came to his senses," or "came to himself." His awakening is the turning point in his life. Another well known story from the Book of Luke is entitled the Rich Man and Lazarus.[72] Here it seems too late for the rich man to gain heaven, but he asks that his brothers be offered the opportunity to wake up and live differently for their souls' sakes.

Key to the experience of forgiveness in any form is waking

up. Jesus from the cross calls for God to forgive those who are involved in his death because they are not aware, not awake. The young man comes to his senses, he wakes up while starving and feeding pigs, and he then makes plans to return home. The rich man seeks guidance for his brothers to wake up to how they are living even though he has lost his opportunity. Becoming aware, becoming conscious of what we are doing and about what we believe, is key to forgiveness.

In terms of self-forgiveness I need to recognise that when I hurt others through my actions or attitudes I have lost the thread of consciousness. I find it helpful at times to stop and ask myself, "What am I doing?" "What was I thinking?" Forgiving others for me begins by recognising that the other also may well have acted unconsciously, just as I am able to do. The Tutu's stress the importance of our shared humanity and here it is critical. My failings, my mistakes, my errors in judgement usually happen when I am not awake, aware or conscious in the present moment. I am therefore at the mercy of my unconscious projection of my needs, desires and fears. It is also so with others. To shift into an awareness of our shared humanity is solid ground for beginning to forgive others and to begin to let go in a positive sense. From this ground we can choose to move forward.

There is another aspect of this dynamic on which I reflect from time to time. I have heard people say that we choose our feelings and responses. No one can force us to feel hurt or injured. This sounds a bit rough, and may not always be the case, but there is an element of truth here to consider. Am I able to understand a person's action toward me in ways other than as some sort of assault on me or rejection of me? Do I have different options for response? Is there one in me who might choose another response other than being hurt or offended? Am I able to glimpse into another's life and get some insight into the choices she or he is making, or is it just about me? Circumstances will vary; I need to be willing to consider as best I can how other people respond to me. I remember a saying that is attributed to Native American wisdom that went like this: "Do not judge another's life until you have walked a mile in his moccasins." My ability to forgive others by whom I feel wounded is grounded in my acceptance of our shared humanity, our oneness.

What about being forgiven by others? Some years ago I worked with a man with whom I had a troubled relationship. It was good and productive in some ways, but it was hard work and at times I conducted myself badly. The work dynamic did lead me into a therapeutic relationship for some time, and in that way it served me well. I left that job after four years and was relieved to do so. Several years later, I decided, with the counsel of an older man I admired, to write a letter of apology for my share of the trouble we endured. I did so and received a warm letter of gratitude and support in return. I took it as an acceptance of my apology, as forgiveness, even though the letter did not address any of the issues we had faced. For me, the exchange of letters created a closure that was satisfactory and I "let it go."

How then do I accept the forgiveness of others? First again, I have to acknowledge and accept that there has been some offence or hurt that I have caused. In my self-reflection on the troubled relationship I have mentioned I needed to come to understand that I had at times acted badly and needed to apologise. Second, I needed to take action, and in this case a letter was most appropriate since we now lived in different countries. I sent the letter, and while I hoped for a positive response, I was clear that I had no control over this. As it turns out I did receive that warm letter that I took as forgiveness, and I accepted this as forgiveness and closure.

In another instance some years ago, a person contacted me to address some of my behaviours in our interactions. It was clear that he was deeply hurt by me. We met face to face and I listened to his story and made no response except to apologise without reservation. In this instance the person did not feel able to forgive me at that time, so I was left to sort out in my mind a closure based on having listened and apologised unreservedly. We did not meet again.

I find this aspect of forgiveness very complex. There have been times when I have hurt others in one way or another. These events of hurt do vary in depth and intensity. The journey toward receiving forgiveness begins with my choosing to become aware of and to accept this fact: I have hurt someone. The action forward in some instances can be direct, like the letter from a distance, or a personal meeting and conversation. In instances of lesser intensity or experiences in close relationships, as in the misunderstandings that happened from time to time in my relationship with Shirley, the action may be to listen, and engage in a lingering hug, sometimes accompanied by some quiet words and or just a deep sigh. At times I have found that the bond of love and attachment seems to create a space in which two people with regard for each other are able to move forward past these events with relative ease.

In offering an apology I may desire and even request forgiveness, it is not mine to expect, require or demand. It is out of my control and up to the other to choose that path or not. My action is in making apology. What form a closure will take depends on the response I receive. Further interaction with the injured person depends on the mutual desires of the people involved. Forgiveness does not always include reconciliation.

Accept, reflect and act, these three movements are essential to the experience of forgiving and being forgiven. With these is the ongoing awareness of our shared humanity, and the fact that at times we wound others and others wound us. The way forward summons me to a certain humility and vulnerability to accept what has transpired, to reflect on my share of the story, and to create a path of action forward.

In this highly complex and confusing area of forgiveness, there are two matters that seem essential for me. The first is to affirm our shared humanity and to keep the playing field level. I keep returning to the poet Terence: "I am a human being, I consider nothing that is human alien to me." We are all wounded at times, we are complex, contradictory, confusing to ourselves, and we are also gifted, extraordinary, ordinary people. As my colleague, Alan Jones once declared: "Human life is messy," and so it is. Gandhi reminds us that we are all one. This is the framework in which our wounding and forgiving takes place.

The second concern is that going forward is ultimately the critical step. Whether the forgiveness is for myself or for others, or for me from others, it is essential to find some way toward a resolution of some kind, whether shared or individual, and to move forward. *Forgiving is at the core of nonviolent living.* I am aware again of the importance of making a decision, a choice. Moving forward is a choice. To hold on to past injuries, to cling to the pain of wounding, to refuse to forgive or be forgiven, is to risk getting stuck in the past, and backing into life, so to speak. The story of Lot's wife comes to mind from the Biblical book of Genesis,[73] It did not serve her at all to keep looking back. Life, like it or not, moves forward relentlessly. *Loving is the most important human action; forgiving is at the core of nonviolent living.* I am challenged once again to continue the discipline of ongoing self-reflection and inner work.

CHAPTER EIGHT

Justpeace is my ongoing hope: mercy tempers the passion of justice.

I encountered the word *"justpeace"*[74] in John Paul Lederach's, *The Moral Imagination*, and found it to my liking. For me it expands the notion of peace as more of a process than a fixed state. Harrison Owen takes the same point of view in his work, *The Practice of Peace.*[75] To have justpeace as a goal includes the intention and commitment to consider all aspects of any situation or relationship in working for a resolution. It is not a matter of "power over," but power shared or the empowerment of those involved. The focus of my vocation and work is the inner life; I refer to this as the psycho-spiritual dimension of life. In the realm of peacebuilding and nonviolence, while I have lots of opinions, I do not experience myself as skilled to speak with any substantial authority and insight into the socio-political frame of our shared lives. I have colleagues I value highly who do this well, and I count on them to counsel and guide me as we go along. Conversely others often ask for my reflections and counsel on the inner way, the somewhat mysterious realm of the psycho-spiritual – the land of the soul. To say it another way, I tend to live primarily in the underworld.

For me, the notion of justpeace has a psycho-spiritual as well as a socio-political application. In terms of my inner life, just-peace involves my effort to face squarely the complexity of my soul, my inner village, and to make every effort to listen to the diverse opinions and attitudes that arise. At times this means engaging patiently the chaos and conflicts of my inner soulscape. Resolution is often not achieved easily for me, and often the conflicts and chaos of any given situation simply must be navigated slowly and endured. Sometimes the resolution involves a change of my conscious attitude in accepting the ongoing nature of diverse points of view, rather than hoping for some tidy and clear decision. The experience of ambivalence is never far away. As John O'Donohue states, we are not simple, singular selves.[76] This takes me back to the way of the cross, and challenges me to make *a voluntary sacrifice* in the interests of inclusive self-love. The sacrifice is to let go of the need to have a quick decision, a tidy answer or a simple, single self-image. To have peace with justice I need to learn to embrace my complexity and ambivalence, and to carry my diversity with care. I also need to realise that when decisions are required, some of my needs and desires or opinions will not be met. The task of justpeace is to listen with care and respect, to accept the various perspectives of villagers, and to decide how to be in the world with a sense of honour for my diverse inner family. O'Donohue, in the same place noted above, says it well: "We cannot embody in action the multiplicity of selves we encounter in our most inward meditations."[76] He goes on to say that we are impoverished as people if we do not acknowledge our many inner selves, and we do ourselves harm if we try to reduce ourselves to a sense of the simple, singular self. Justpeace with myself is navigating daily my complexity, and learning to carry consciously my chaos. Justpeace implies a hope for wholeness as it inspires me to be inclusive, to welcome all of me inwardly and to choose consciously how to act outwardly. I intuit that it also cultivates energy for resilience in that our disciplined inner work has the potential to fuel a hope that looks forward. The inner work of justpeace is informed by compassion. Compassion – to suffer with – invites me to suffer myself at times as I carry my many different responses to daily life. As humbling as it can be, it is also empowering as it represents an honest self-understanding.

Both in the realms of inner work and of outer action, *justpeace is our ongoing hope*. Hope is crucial in sustaining a nonviolent way of life for ourselves and with others. On reflection I think I have underestimated, or perhaps never really understood, the contribution of hope to my life. That said, what else gets me out of bed each day?

At a presentation in 1980 in Los Angeles, my colleague Alan Jones expressed another provocative one liner. He asserted: "We are more defined by our future than by our past."[77] In a world in which we are often inclined to define ourselves by our past, especially our childhood experiences, this is a startling declaration. Yet in the sacred texts of my faith tradition I notice that the movement of the Divine Spirit leads us forward. In the Biblical story of the Exodus we read that the Lord went in front of the people in the forms of a pillar of cloud by day and a pillar of fire by night.[78] In the Biblical story of Jesus' temptations, we read that the Spirit led Jesus out into the wilderness.[79] I am not a scholar of Hebrew, but I was told years ago that the Name of God revealed to Moses in the story of the burning bush in Exodus, chapter 3, may be translated not only as "I am who I am," but also as "I will be who I will be".[80] The energy of divinity often leads from the front and moves forward. In my vocation for my life, I am called, led, summoned relentlessly into my future. Again it is a matter of both-and. While we are deeply impacted by our past, we are daily challenged to face forward into our own unique destinies. As I see it at present, hope fuels my resilience and enables me to face forward in my life. Yes, it does get me out of bed in the morning, wondering what the day will bring in spite of my plans. Hope gives me courage to be faithful to my vision for my life. Hope energises me to continue to put flesh on my aspirations. In the core of my struggles with depression, anxiety and addiction, there has been, and continues to be, the energy of hope nudging me forward, sometimes one step at a time. This hope is an optimism tempered by honest realism that grows out of the deep inner conversations and broodings for a justpeace – coherence in the midst of chaos, and thoughtful, considered action emerging from endless complexity. Both inwardly and outwardly there are times when justpeace cannot lead to resolution, rather some dynamic tensions must be carried with care. We live with brokenness, not all things can be healed or resolved. Yet we hold to the hope of justpeace.

Mercy tempers the passion of justice. In a recent conversation my colleague Tom Gannon shared a line he heard in a sermon. The speaker said, "We want justice for others, we want mercy for ourselves." It may be secretly attractive, but in the long run it won't work. If we hope for mercy for ourselves then we are honour bound to extend the same to others.

While we hold ideally to the notion that justice is blind, I am not so convinced. It seems to me that justice is not blind or impartial, but is interpreted by those who administer it. More than once I have heard people declare that the outcome of a legal process depends on the judge and jury in the specific instance. Justice gets interpreted subjectively through people, and it may be here that mercy is expressed, in the context of our shared humanity.

What then of the mercy that tempers justice? The idea of mercy, of being merciful, brings to mind compassion, a kindly spirit, generosity, acting with care and love beyond any concepts of deserving. Mercy springs from a heart that knows its own wounds and failings. Mercy lives on a level playing field. Mercy knows that I, too, have feet of clay. If I am able to embrace and learn through my suffering, this learning can become the fuel that ignites and drives my capacity for mercy. Mercy calls for account-ability in context, a situational approach to our understanding. Again the question framed in mercy: What is the loving thing to do? It is the task of mercy to soften the hard edges of justice, and to hold justice and mercy in creative tension in the larger context of love.

How am I with myself? In terms of my inner life it is mercy that gives some ease from my self-judgement and shame. In the face of any transgression mercy makes it possible for me to forgive myself and to accept my failings. This mercy helps me step down from the pedestal of my delusions of superiority and to stand among others as both a unique and ordinary person. It is this merciful compassion for ourselves that enables our commitment to reflect continually on how we are living with ourselves, accepting our limits and engaging the summons to step more fully into our own lives. From the compassion of mercy I am enabled to live more openly with others in a communion of equality, a commu-nity of shared humanity, in which I know well, with Terence the Roman playwright, that if a human being can do it, so can I. It is mercy that enables me to live in this community of wonderfully gifted and remarkably ordinary people. Gandhi again: We are one. This mercy, this compassion, this self-love, these describe the core energy that makes it possible for us to sustain a nonviolent way of life. *Justpeace is our ongoing hope; mercy tempers the passion of justice.*

Afterword

Some years ago I facilitated a conference on peace. We did an exercise together wherein we lined up chronologically according to the year in which peace became for us a living, personal concern. This was a take off on an exercise I had seen my colleague Brendan McKeague facilitate some years earlier. From our "years" we shared our stories, and before we moved on I asked the participants to look at their feet and to reflect silently on where our feet were placed. It is another way of reflecting on that for which I stand.

In the historical novel, *The Paris Library*, Dorothy Reeder, is the Directress of the American Library in Paris. During the Nazi occupation of Paris she was determined to keep the library open to serve its subscribers, including the Jewish people who were banned from entering the premises. She reflects on her decision: "You're nothing without principles. Nowhere without ideals. No one without courage."[81]

This review of my principles has been about reflecting for myself on that for which I stand, it is about trying to understand how the principles I crafted ten years ago had been growing up in me over many years. "How did I get here?" The title question has driven the work. It has been a journey of crafting over many months. Sometimes the words have flowed easily, at others times I have had to walk away for days on end waiting for something to move me, or push me forward. I come to these final words with a deep sense of satisfaction, knowing as well that the journey is far more complex and chaotic at times than it is coherent. I feel more in touch with myself, and yet in many ways remain ever a mystery to me.

For any who read this I hope it is a provocation. I have told the story of the encounter with Professor Pitika Ntali in Johannesburg now several years ago, in which he described the project of his large black granite sculptures on the history of apartheid not as a memorial, but as a provocation. He wanted people to reflect, to think about what had happened and to be provoked by the memory of this history. I take my word from him and his passion for self-reflection. My hope is that any who review what I have shared will be provoked to reflect with some discipline on where their feet are placed, to become more fully themselves and to have some useful insight and response to the question: "How did I get here?" I am convinced that when we identify our principles and ideals, then we can claim the courage to live with conscious intention for the common good.

Endnotes

Introduction

1. Quoist, Michel. 1963. *Prayers.* p.23.
2. Jung, Carl G. 1961. *Memories, Dreams, Reflections.* p. 4.
3. It is found in The Hymnal of the Protestant Episcopal Church of the United States of America, 1940, in number 519, stanza 3.
4. The passage is at 1 Corinthians 13:11.
5. Keyes, Jr., Kenneth S. 1950. *How To Develop Your Thinking Ability.* I have found this a very useful resource over decades.
6. Verwoerd, Wilhelm. n.d. *Can peace be "built"? Metaphors for peace practice.*

First Principle
The divine spirit is the life energy of all that is: all life is interconnected

7. Kelly, Thomas. 1941. *A Testament of Devotion.* p. 29.
8. James, William. 1902/1985. *The Varieties of Religious*

Experience. p. 508. Lecture XX, "Conclusions," contains the idea of the MORE.

9. The Dog series of eighteen active imagination experiences took place from 1979-1981 and later was a part of my PhD research exploring the relationship between active imagination and Christian religious experience.

10. I encountered a list of Gandhi's principles in the Pace e Bene workbook *Engage*, and later Googled the topic to find that there are several lists of principles attributed to Gandhi.

11. Dallett, Janet. 2008, *Listening to the Rhino.* pp. 2-4.

12. Jung, Carl. G. in Sabini, Meredith. 2002, 2005, 2008. *The Earth Has a Soul.* p. 207.

13. Oliver, Mary. 2016. *Upstream.* "Upstream", p. 5 and "Winter Hours" p. 154.

14. Kunzig, Robert. November 2020. *National Geographic.* "Let's Not Waste This Moment." p. 78.

15. Obama, Barack. 2020. *A Promised Land.* p. 15.

16. I found the quote on one of Adrian Steirn's websites. His photographic and film work are dramatic and inspiring tributes to both people and animals, and his sites are well worth a visit.

17. Hollis, James. 1996. *Swamplands of the Soul.* pp. 33-34.

18. Macy, Joanna and Johnstone, Chris. 2012. *Active Hope.* p. 5ff.

19. I met Alan when he was on the faculty of The General Seminary in New York City. From 1980-1985 we offered regional training programs for spiritual directors across the USA. He was later the Dean of Grace Cathedral in San Francisco. In my memory he was famous for one-liners in his presentations that seemed to arise spontaneously.

20. Sacks, Jonathan. 2002/2003. *The Dignity of Difference.* pp. 4-5.

Second Principle
At the heart of all life there is mystery:
there are many truths I do not know

21. Henry Miller, in Dallett, Janet. 2008. *Listening to The Rhino.* p. 25.
22. See the Biblical books Matthew 17:1-8; Mark 9:2-8 and Luke 9:28-36.
23. Moore, Thomas. 1992. *Care of the Soul.* This is a remarkable guide to the soul and soul work.
24. Baird, Julia, 2020. *Phosphorescence.* p. 265.
25. Hollis, James. 2007. *Why Good People Do Bad Things.* p. 36. For those interested in Jung's concept of the Shadow, this is a "must-read."
26. Jung, Carl. G. 1973. *Letters*, Vol 1. p. 375.
27. Doerr, Anthony. 2010. "The River Nemunas." in *Memory Wall.* p. 185.

Third Principle
My call is to live my life in this larger spirit life and mystery:
wholeness, nor perfection, is my hope

28. Kelsey, Morton. 1983. *Reaching.* pp. 42 ff.
29. Hollis, James. 2003. *On This Journey We Call Our Life.* pp. 57ff. I have found James Hollis very helpful here, especially his chapter, "What is my Vocation?"
30. O'Donohue, John. 1998. *Eternal Echoes.* London: Bantam Books. pp. 365.
31. The Biblical book of Matthew, 6:24.
32. Commins, Gary. 2015. *If Only We Could See:* pp 357ff. I first

encountered this phrase in Gary's work, who explores it in interfaith contexts.

33. Tutu, Desmond. 2007. "Introduction." *Peace: The Words and Inspiration of Mahatma Gandhi*. There are also various internet sources for the word, "Ubuntu."

34. Jung, Carl. G. (1932/1958). "Psychotherapists or the Clergy." In *The Collected Works of C. G. Jung*. p. 339, para. 519.

35. McBride, Terry. (1997). "Forward." In *Dreamworks*. p.xi.

36. Haig, Matt. *The Midnight Library*. 2020. p. 127. The resources on Google are extensive and offer different points of view as to the reliability of Dunbar's proposal. In reference to concerns for wholeness and inclusivity, the work provides a useful insight.

Fourth Principle
All creation is my family:
I was born into community

37. O'Donohue, John. 1998. *Eternal Echoes*. p. 366.

38. Tutu, Desmond and Mpho. 2014. *The Book of Forgiving*. p. 126.

39. Davis, Wade. 2009. *The Wayfinders*. p. 18.

40. Thomas Aquinas, "The Mandate." in *Love Poems from God*. p. 127.

41. Teresa of Avila, "When the Holy Thaws." in *Love Poems from God*. pp. 290f.

42. Robert Jones, Jr. 2021. *The Prophets*. page 162.

Fifth Principle
My inner work shapes my outer life:
what I do not engage within I project onto others

43. Among the many resources for dreams and dream work, here are three. Sanford, John. *Dreams: God's Forgotten Language.* Johnson, Robert. *Inner Work. Dreams.* A podcast I made for the "On the Way" series at St. John's Anglican Cathedral in Brisbane, Australia.https://omny.fm/shows/on-the-way/on-the-way-dreams-with-george-trippe

44. Trippe, George E. 2000. *Active Imagination and Christian Religious Experience:* The thesis is in the library archives at Edith Cowan University, Perth, Australia. I also have composed a manuscript on Active Imagination in 2020, entitled, *Who Said That? The Spirited Practice of Active Imagination.* Robert Johnson's book, *Inner Work,* mentioned above, is a classic on both dreams and active imagination.

45. McBride, Terry. (1997). "Forward." In Dreamworks. p.xi.

46. The Biblical book of Matthew, 5:44

47. There are excellent works on the Shadow available, including Hollis' work mentioned under principle two. In the podcast series mentioned above, I have recorded an interview on the Shadow: https://omny.fm/shows/on-the-way/on-the-way-making-peace-with-the-shadow?in_playlist=on-the-way!podcast

48. Terence. (Publius Terentius Afer). Internet Source: PoemHunter.com.

49. Francis of Assisi, "Humility and Compassion." in *Love Poems from God.* p. 37.

50. Powell, Jim. 2010. *The Breaking of Eggs.* pp. 198-9.

51. The Biblical book of Luke, 10:27.

52. Mandela, Nelson. 2010. *Nelson Mandela: Conversations with Myself.* p. 7.
53. Hafiz, in *Love Poems from God.* p. 159.

Sixth Principle
The way of the cross is the journey to wholeness: it is the path of love

54. Davis, Wade. 2009. *The Wayfinders.* p. 130.
55. The Biblical book of John, 12:24.
56. Jung Carl. G. 1958/1980. "Jung and Religious Belief." In *The Collected Works of C. G. Jung.* Volume 18. pp. 702-44. para. 1584-1690.
57. As above, para. 1661.
58. Johnson, Robert. 1991. *Owning Your Own Shadow.* p. 107.
59. Commins, Gary. 2015. *If Only We Could See.* p. 265.
60. Borg, Marcus. 2003. *The Heart of Christianity.* pp. 28ff.
61. Rohr, Richard. 2004. *Adam's Return.* p. 60.

Seventh Principle
Loving is the most important human action: forgiving is at the core of nonviolent living

62. Kelsey, Morton. 1989. *Reaching.* pp. 102-03.
63. Johnson. Robert A. with Jerry M. Ruhl. 1998. *Balancing Heaven and Earth.* p. 59.
64. Rabia, "The Way the Forest Shelters." in *Love Poems from God.* p. 14.
65. Hafiz, in *I Heard God Laughing.* p. 43.

66. Barnes, Julian. 2018. *The Only Story.* p. 3.
67. Tutu, Desmond and Mpho. 2014. *The Book of Forgiving.*
68. Lucy Radcliffe speaking to Leonard Gilbert in Morton, Kate. 2018. *The Clockmaker's Daughter.* p. 302
69. Tutu, Desmond. 2007. "Introduction" to *Peace: The Words and Inspiration of Mahatma Gandhi.* p. 3.
70. The statement here is from the Biblical Book of Luke, 32:34. It is not found in all early texts of Luke or in the other three Gospel books. Under the reference, "the seven sayings of Jesus from the cross," Wikipedia offers a diagram of sources for each of the seven.
71. From the Biblical book of Luke, 15:11-32. Some entitle this "The Prodigal and his Elder Brother." Years ago, I read that Dr. Joachim Jeremias suggested the title is more appropriately, "The Loving Father," as the father is the key actor in the story.
72. The Biblical Book of Luke, 16:19-31. Some sources have named the rich man as Dives.
73. The story is in the Biblical book of Genesis, chapter 19.

Eighth Principle
Justpeace is my ongoing hope: mercy tempers the passion of justice

74. Lederach, John Paul. 2005. *The Moral Imagination.* p. 22. See also the Glossary, p. 182.
75. Owen, Harrison. 2003. *The Practice of Peace.*
76. O'Donohue, John. 1997. *Anam Cara.* p. 113.
77. Alan made this observation at the first regional training program for spiritual directors that we co-facilitated. When

I asked him about what he meant, he did not remember having said it. He was inspired when he got fired up.

78. The Biblical book of Exodus, 13:21-22.
79. The Biblical book of Matthew, 4:1.
80. The Biblical book of Exodus, 3:14.

Afterword

81. Charles, Janet Skeslien. 2021. *The Paris Library*. p. 175.

References

All Biblical references are from the *New Revised Standard Version*. 1989. New York. Oxford University Press.

Baird, Julia, 2020. *Phosphorescence*. Sydney: HarperCollins*Publishers*.

Barnes, Julian. 2018. *The Only Story*. London: Jonathan Cape.

Borg, Marcus. 2003. *The Heart of Christianity: Rediscovering a Life of Faith*.
New York: HarperSanFrancisco.

Charles, Janet Skeslien. 2021. *The Paris Library*. London: Two Roads.

Commins, Gary. 2015. *If Only We Could See: Mystical Vision and Social Transformation*. Eugene: Cascade Books.

Dallett, Janet. 2008, *Listening to the Rhino: Violence and Healing in a Scientific Age*. New York: Pleasure Boat Studio.

Davis, Wade. 2009. *The Wayfinders: Why Ancient Wisdom Matters in the Modern World*. Toronto: House of Anansi Press, Inc.

Doerr, Anthony. 2010. "The River Nemunas." in *Memory Wall*. London: 4th Estate.

Francis of Assisi, "Humility and Compassion." in *Love Poems from God: Twelve Sacred Voices from the East and West*. Trans: Daniel Ladinsky. 2002. New York: Penguin Compass.

Hafiz, "I Have Come Into the World to See This." in *Love Poems from God: Twelve Sacred Voices from the East and West.* Trans: Daniel Ladinsky. 2002. New York: Penguin Compass.

Hafiz, "I Know the Way You Can Get" in *I Heard God Laughing: Poems of Hope and Joy.* Renderings of HAFIZ, by Daniel Ladinsky. 2006. New York: Penguin Books,

Haig, Matt. 2020. *The Midnight Library.* Edinburgh: Canongate Books Ltd.

Hollis, James. 1996. *Swamplands of the Soul: New Life in Dismal Places.* Toronto: Inner City Books.

Hollis, James. 2003. *On This Journey We Call Our Life: Living the Questions.* Toronto: Inner City Books.

Hollis, James. 2007. *Why Good People Do Bad Things: Understanding Our Darker Selves.* New York: Gotham Books.

James, William. 1902/1985. *The Varieties of Religious Experience.* New York: Penguin Books.

Johnson, Robert. 1986. *Inner Work: Using Dreams and Active Imagination for Personal Growth.* New York: HarperSanFrancisco.

Johnson, Robert. 1991. *Owning Your Own Shadow: Understanding the Dark Side of the Psyche.* New York: HarperSanFrancisco.

Johnson. Robert A. with Jerry M. Ruhl. 1998. *Balancing Heaven and Earth: A Memoir.* New York: HarperSanFrancisco.

Jones, Jr. Robert. 2021. *The Prophets* London: Riverrun, Quercus Editions Ltd.

Jung, Carl. G. 1932/1958. Psychotherapists or the Clergy. In *The Collected Works of C. G. Jung.* R. F. C. Hull, Trans. Vol. 11. Princeton: Princeton University Press.

Jung Carl. G. 1958/1980. Jung and Religious Belief. In *The Collected Works of C. G. Jung* (R. F. C. Hull, Trans.) Princeton: Princeton University Press. Volume 18.

Jung, Carl G. 1961. *Memories, Dreams, Reflections.* Aniela Jaffe, Ed. New York: Pantheon Books.

Jung, Carl. G. 1973. *Letters,* Vol 1. Gerhard Adler, Ed. R. F. C. Hull, Trans. London: Routledge & Kegan Paul.

Jung Carl. G. in Sabini, Meredith. 2002, 2005, 2008. *The Earth Has a Soul: C. G. Jung on Nature, Technology & Modern Life.* Berkeley: North Atlantic Books.

Kelly, Thomas. 1941. *A Testament of Devotion.* New York: Harper & Row.

Kelsey, Morton. 1983. *Reaching: The Journey to Fulfilment.* San Francisco: Harper & Row.

Keyes, Jr., Kenneth S. 1950. *How To Develop Your Thinking Ability: A Guide to Sound Decisions.* New York: McGraw-Hill Book Company, Inc.

Kunzig, Robert. 2020. "Let's Not Waste This Moment." in *National Geographic.* November 2020.

Lederach, John Paul. 2005. *The Moral Imagination: The Art and Soul of Building Peace.* New York: Oxford University Press.

McBride, Terry. 1997. Forward. In *Dreamworks: A meeting of Spirituality and Psychology.* Steve Price and David Haynes. Blackburn: HarperCollins*Religious.*

Macy, Joanna and Johnstone, Chris. 2012. *Active Hope.* Sydney: Finch Publishing.

Mandela, Nelson. 2010. *Nelson Mandela: Conversations with Myself.* London: Macmillan.

Moore, Thomas. 1992. *Care of the Soul: A Guide for Cultivating Depth and Sacredness in Everyday Life.* New York: HarperPerennial.

Morton, Kate. 2018. *The Clockmaker's Daughter.* Crows Nest NSW. Allen & Unwin.

O'Donohue, John. 1997. *Anam Cara: A Book of Celtic Wisdom.* New York: Harper Perennial.

O'Donohue, John. 1998. *Eternal Echoes: Exploring our Hunger to Belong.* London: Bantam Books.

Obama, Barack. 2020. *A Promised Land.* London: Viking.

Oliver, Mary. 2016. *Upstream: Selected Essays.* New York: Penguin Press.

Owen, Harrison. 2003. *The Practice of Peace.* Published by Open Space Institutes.

Powell, Jim. 2010. *The Breaking of Eggs.* London: Weidenfeld & Nicolson.

Quoist, Michel. 1963. *Prayers.* Trans. Agnes M. Forsyth and Anne Marie de Commaille. New York: Sheed And Ward.

Rabia, "The Way the Forest Shelters," in *Love Poems from God: Twelve Sacred Voices from the East and West.* Trans: Daniel Ladinsky. 2002. New York: Penguin Compass.

Rohr, Richard. 2004. *Adam's Return: The Five Promises of Male Initiation.*

New York: The Crossroads Publishing Company.

Sacks, Jonathan. 2002/2003. *The Dignity of Difference: How to Avoid the Clash of Civilizations.* London: Continuum.

Sanford, John. 1968, 1989. *Dreams: God's Forgotten Language.* New York: HarperSanFrancisco.

Steirn, Adrian. See: https://www.adriansteirn.com

Terence. (Publius Terentius Afer). n.d. Internet Source: PoemHunter.com

Teresa of Avila. "When the Holy Thaws." in *Love Poems from God: Twelve Sacred Voices from the East and West.* Trans: Daniel Ladinsky. 2002. New York: Penguin Compass.

Thomas Aquinas. "The Mandate." in *Love Poems from God: Twelve Sacred Voices from the East and West.* Trans: Daniel Ladinsky. 2002. New York: Penguin Compass.

Trippe, George E. 2018. *Dreams.* "On the Way" podcast series at St. John's Anglican Cathedral in Brisbane, Australia. https://omny.fm/shows/on-the-way/on-the-way-dreams-with-george-trippe

Trippe, George E. 2000. *Active Imagination and Christian Religious Experience: A Study in Relationship.* Edith Cowan University Library. Perth, Australia.

Trippe, George E. 2020. *Making Peace with the Shadow.* "On the Way" podcast series at St. John's Anglican Cathedral in Brisbane, Australia. https://omny.fm/shows/on-the-way/on-the-way-making-peace-with-the-shadow?in_playlist=on-the-way!podcast

Trippe, George E. 2022. *Who Said That? The Spirited Practice of Active Imagination.* Manuscript in process of publication.

Tutu, Desmond. 2007. Introduction. *Peace: The Words and Inspiration of Mahatma Gandhi.* Sydney: Hachette.

Tutu, Desmond and Mpho. 2014. *The Book of Forgiving.* London: WilliamCollins.

Verwoerd, Wilhelm. n.d. *Can peace be "built"? Metaphors for peace practice.* Glencree Working Paper No. 1: Glencree Co., Wicklow, Ireland Glencree Centre for Peace and Reconciliation. Email: wilhelm.verwoerd@gmail.com

Acknowledgements

I developed these eight principles while on the facilitation team for the peace education program, Nonviolent Interfaith Leadership under the auspices of Pace e Bene Australia, a peace education community. We three facilitators, Stacie Chappell, Brendan McKeague and I, developed six principles as the foundation for our program. To our surprise and amusement, it was an exercise that took far more time than we had anticipated. After we had completed our work, I went on to develop the eight principles here for myself. Several colleagues and friends have read and commented on this work at various stages along the way and I am grateful for our conversations and their encouragement. In addition to Stacie and Brendan, these include Gary Commins, Ann Morgan, Wilhelm Verwoerd, Louis Papaelias, Adrian Pizzata, Timothy McInnes, Dom Fay and Stephen Harrison. I have received invaluable support in conversations over lunches with Marie Isaacson who has encouraged me to value what I offer, and to enjoy the process. For these and many, many others over a long period of time, I am grateful. I am also grateful to Ann Wilson at Independent Ink, and her colleagues

Michelle Van Dyk and Julian Mole for their focused attention to detail and their collaboration, counsel and guidance in bringing my vision for this work to production. In the time of Covid they have persevered to produce the book and have also given me a great learning experience. It's been a pleasure.